In
the Time
of
Coronavirus

In
the Time
of
Coronavirus

Reflecting on the Past to Embrace
a Joyful Future

Janet Zinn, LCSW

atmosphere press

For Larry with gratitude

Introduction

I had been a mental health provider for less than three years when I was called to work as a trauma specialist following 9/11. I was a New York psychotherapist who had trained in trauma counseling and was able to join the teams of national and international trauma counselors who came to New York City to work with victims' family members, witnesses, first responders, and survivors of the terrorist attacks. So, when the pandemic hit, I had twenty-five years of experience in working with trauma and loss. This comprehensive background provided a perspective on living through and supporting others in surviving the global health crisis.

I created a weekly blog to normalize our collective experiences while speaking of my observations and sharing self-care tips. The blog posts were personal in nature. I thought it was important to normalize what we were experiencing collectively, and what we were going through personally. It is a subjective record of those times, imperfect in nature and reflecting our flawed humanity. Imperfect since we were all in uncertain spaces doing our best to navigate unprecedented events. And, imperfect because I returned to familiar themes again and again. I repeat self-care tips because they worked for me time after time. I found it was important to include self-care tips, because I heard from clients that they were at a loss as to how to get through their days and weeks with such strong emotions.

In the Time of Coronavirus is the compilation of these blog posts with photographs I started taking the second week of March 2020. Each post is its own short chapter. I chose to share the blog posts as a book after attending a performance of Suzan-Lori Parks's brilliant musical theater piece, "Plays for the Plague Year," in which she documented each day with a short play. It was so inspiring. I saw the healing power of looking back on the shared days, weeks, months, and years we all endured. **In the Time of Coronavirus** recalls what we all went through, acknowledging readers' ongoing courage and inner resources. And it provides many self-care tips that can be curated to fit each reader's life going forward.

It is my hope that you read **In the Time of Coronavirus** as a resource, a reflection, a remembrance, self-help, support, or in any way that is right for you.

WEEK ONE:
Self-Care Versus Scare Care

The news can be frightening. Our extra-curricular activities, a good number of which provide joy, are canceled. In many ways, we are left to our own devices to uplift our moods at a time when the odds are against us. Anxiety is up, and tools to fight depression are down. We are living through a global crisis. You can check the World Health Organization for recommendations on how to navigate this new reality. And, to care for yourself mentally and emotionally, here are a few things to know while semi-isolated yet virtually bonded by this pandemic.

First, look to see if your mood is calibrated by fears and anxiety or by compassion and kindness. We may all feel fearful. It's natural to have some level of anxiety when faced with the unknown. At other times we live in the illusion that we can control our environment, but now, we're faced with the fact that we don't always have complete control in our world. Lack of control or feelings of powerlessness leave us vulnerable. And many of us may feel fearful of that vulnerability. Add to that the many warnings viewed on the media stoking our fears, and we can feel like a hot mess.

In times like this, there's a simple exercise. Close your eyes and think of a good friend, either real or imagined, who is patient, kind, and compassionate. Then see yourself as that friend. You can open your eyes, becoming the friend you've conceived.

How would you treat a friend who might be scared? What would you tell them? Tell yourself those things. Be a good friend to yourself. Write down anything that might bear repeating, something like "slow down," or "read a poem that gives you solace."

It's important to know that feeling afraid at this time is natural. In fact, some news outlets count on it since fear sells. Fear is a most contagious symptom. Limiting your fear, or stepping away from fear and anxiety, allows us to enjoy small moments like seeing the sunrise when few people are out and about, or laughing with a loved one.

Another short exercise you can try is lightly closing your eyes, putting your feet firmly on the floor if you're sitting, and doing a body scan from your head down. See what physical sensations you experience. Mentally identify them. For instance, tightness in my jaw, tension in my shoulders, and butterflies in my stomach area. It brings us into the here and now and allows us to focus on specific physical manifestations of anxiety.

A tried-and-true exercise is to sit in a quiet place and uncross your hands and legs. Close your eyes. Then, starting at your feet, tighten and release the muscles. Move up your body, tightening and releasing isolated muscles until you pass your forehead. Finally, tighten and release all muscles in your body at once. It will help to loosen you up substantially.

In addition to anxiety, depressive symptoms might arise. If you're able, seek professional help. Have virtual sessions with your psychotherapist, use a therapy app if a therapist isn't available to you, and reach out to your support system. Join online groups for solidarity.

Other resources to soothe yourself are online art galleries and museums. You can look up the art you love, or Travel and Leisure is a wonderful resource that can take you on a global art tour. Another delightful diversion and awe-inspiring site is one created by the indomitable Laura Benanti. She encouraged high school performers to create videos of the solos they haven't been able to perform at their school musicals since public gatherings have been suspended. Check it out on Instagram. YouTube is also a perfect source for performances, speeches, talks, old commercials, tutorials, and instructions. I have gone to YouTube for Judy Garland and Barbra Streisand singing together, Yoga and Pilates classes, TV theme songs of the 60s, and nature videos, to name a few.

If you're not inclined to explore other avenues of joy, you're not alone. We are more inclined to devolve into old habits when we're stressed. I certainly have found myself cooking and eating comfort foods rather than steamed vegetables. Actually, I rarely, if ever, eat steamed vegetables. I just don't care for them. Nonetheless, this morning I made blender hollandaise sauce to cover my eggs. I haven't done that in years. Oh boy, did I enjoy it. Some of us may become more reactive, quick to anger. Others may bake or cook and eat comfort foods, like me. Still others may go for another glass of wine. While others may binge-watch more TV while we're unable to visit our offices. And the list goes on. Remember to have compassion. Enjoy it if you go there. Be aware of its impact on others. Compassion and patience for ourselves are imperative as we find we're acting in ways that don't thrill us. We can try to remember that this is a time-limited experience. We will move on, and we always have the next moment to make another choice. Or we can implement kindness for ourselves and others by appreciating that we are beyond our capacity to make a change now. We can know that we've made changes in the past, and we will do so again if we so choose.

Remember to reach out to others. Being able to speak with those who support us is invaluable. We can reach out to volunteer, when possible. Or we can reach out to ask for help. That may take courage. And courage is exactly what is called for now. Let's support one another to get through this unique historical moment.

Fear & Other Options

I went to Central Park yesterday for a walk, keeping a safe distance from others. While in the park, I found unpopulated paths and was happy to enjoy the brisk, sunny day on my own. Yet, when leaving the park, there was a group of younger people spread out on the walkway and the road. I had to take a wide circle around them to maintain the six feet dictum, certain that others in the park also felt put upon by the group's enjoyment of their time together. It was at that moment that the measures I had taken to stay safe were challenged, and I quickly saw the small clique as my enemy.

I work hard to live with compassion. I confess that sometimes I lean towards snarkiness and criticism. And, though I appreciated that they needed each other just as much as I needed to distance myself, I realized that I was more afraid

9

of the Coronavirus than I had realized. I was judging them for being socially irresponsible for their public choice to bond together. I don't think I was wrong in my judgment, but I know that seeing others as the enemy stems from my fears.

So many of us are afraid. A good number of us are experiencing heightened anxiety. It is hard to function well when we are being driven by deep-seated fear. If we are to get through this time, we may be best served to see what's in front of us, moment by moment. I'm not much of a driver, but I do know what it's like to drive in a deep fog or a hard snowstorm. To stay the course, we have to look closely at the small sliver of visible road beyond our windshield while we continue to breathe. Understanding that we will reach our destination eventually. We may have to get off the road to rest. Or we may have to slow down, letting other cars drive by, to inch our way through the malevolent weather. This takes patience and fortitude, two qualities we can call upon during the Coronavirus scare.

We are seeing acts of kindness and generosity on our social media feeds. There are dance parties and free classes. There are meditation sessions, as well as mindfulness exercises being offered. Friends and family are reaching out to connect. The art institutions and individuals who are unable to work, not earning a wage now, are freely providing concerts, platforms, and virtual galleries to serve us. We may be starved of physical contact, but we are being fed a banquet for much of our spiritual and emotional needs.

I am using this time to check in with myself and others. How can I care for myself? And, in what ways do I need to wait? I will wait to dine with friends. I will wait to see new exhibits and shows. In the meantime, I am enjoying books and phone calls, two old-school tools. And, yes, I am old school. I am fortunate to be working, but that means my closets and cupboards are not as tidy as I'd like. And I am okay with that for now. I do know that when I'm critical of myself or others that I'm displacing my fear. Or, perhaps, I'm transferring feelings of sadness, frustration, or other emotions I'm not keen to feel to something more tangible, like my messy living room.

These are difficult times. It can take bravery to get through each day. Rather than feeding the fear, let's acknowledge our courage. Let's be proud of our fortitude. Let us connect not from fear but from compassion. We can acknowledge our worries, and still stay true to who we know ourselves and others to be – caring people who will do our very best to get through this pandemic and its emotional fallout. Let us all strive to be the hero in our own and others' Coronavirus narratives.

Self-Care Tips:

(Tips are suggestions of simple exercises and activities which I've tried myself that may prompt compassion, kindness, joy and care. Only choose those that resonate for you.)

Meditate with others:

- Find free mediation links on apps and online to have a shared mindful experience.

- Find Dance Parties online. Instagram and other platforms feature created dance parties so that you connect through movement with others.

- Find films to watch on travel sites.

- Art: Go online to enjoy the stunning art world. Mental Floss has many links to art museum sites.

- Buy or borrow books from your public library, Audible, or go to your local bookstore website and order a book to be delivered.

WEEK THREE:
Who Are We Now?

We've had a couple of weeks to get used to this new reality we're experiencing. We're learning how to adjust to social distancing and self-quarantines. And, we're learning about ourselves in the process.

We've seen courage in the face of life and death circumstances. We've seen ignorance in the face of scientific facts. And we've seen big-heartedness in the face of financial difficulties.

Yesterday, I enjoyed a short run on the empty promenade in a light mist. When I hit the pavement on York Avenue, the trash was being emptied by smiling sanitation workers. We wished each other well, adding joy to my lone run. They are essential workers, risking their well-being to keep the city running. While I've passed many who have avoided eye contact, the smiles that are shared with strangers have been a needed tonic in these uncertain times.

It's been an interesting couple of months. There is great sadness and loss. Too many have lost lives or their health. And, we all have lost our daily routines. We've lashed out and have been judgmental. Conversely, we've also been kind and caring. And, we are learning how to navigate this time, garnering dormant strengths.

I've doubled down on meditation. I feel like it's been helpful to me and necessary for my family. I can be intolerant when I'm stressed, and no one deserves that now. But, mostly, I've had to give myself and others a pass. I cannot hold myself to unrealistic standards when the world has changed so drastically. Instead, I am coming to know myself in a different way. I'm not laughing as much, but when I do laugh, I am overtaken by tearful glee, seemingly making the most of a rare moment. I make sure to read others' works, particularly those I know. And, I am moved by their natural talents. Music has more power than ever. And how fortunate we are to have such unlimited access. And, though I have spent years going to live shows, theater, museums and galleries, I am extremely grateful that I have the space to rest now. Because I certainly need the downtime. We all have the opportunity to learn more about ourselves than we knew prior to this pandemic. We are changed. Let us all consciously create a change for the better.

Self-Care Tips:

- Take things slowly. No need to rush now.

- Meditate. Even if you focus for one minute, mediation can strengthen your relationship with yourself and the world around you.

- Listen to the music you love.

WEEK FOUR:
Indecision

This is my third try at writing this week's blog post. I started writing about courage, but I am not feeling particularly brave right now. Perhaps that will change, but it would be inauthentic to be a cheering squad with a fake smile. The other subject was how difficult it is to make decisions right now. Even though this blog post is proof of my indecision, I wasn't clear about what to include.

True that during times of stress, our ability to think clearly is compromised. Making decisions during COVID-19 is especially fraught since many of our choices are, in fact, life and death choices. Do I go for a walk? Do I completely quarantine? We all want to weigh in on that, and yet each of us has to make these difficult choices for ourselves. And, in doing so, we impact those who care about us. This is particularly difficult when we don't see eye to eye on this.

And, our decisions, little and big, have an impact on

our relationships, many of which, at least here in New York City, are taking place together in small spaces.

Alex and I are challenged by who will be in the kitchen at any given time since we all want something different, and our cooking space is tiny and narrow. We easily snap at one or the other; then, when I'm surprised at my reaction, I have to backpedal to understand what's really stressing me out, calming myself before providing a genuine apology. I find myself at turns grateful for all I have and questioning myself and others. I'm grateful to have a family who will tolerate my moods. And I am lost at times in a fog, unable to decide to take a nap or clean. Or I'm blaming strangers for not social distancing at least six feet. Or I'm blaming Alex for not cleaning his room so I can theoretically feel calmer. It's not productive, yet there it is. And now it takes me a bit longer to reconnect with myself. I am trying to be patient since the Coronavirus is stressful for all of us. And, as mentioned above, stress changes how we respond to what's in front of us.

So, when we don't know whether we'll go left or right, let's stop, take a breath, and proceed one way or the other. The choices we make may have us worrying, but that is, simply put, a side effect of getting through this pandemic. Our collective challenge is to navigate the emotional waves even though we've never traveled this sea before.

Self-Care Tips:

There has been a lot of focus on our hands, like washing them properly or being conscious of what they are touching. Once they are washed, place your hands on your heart. They are tools for touch and healing. This gives us a moment to experience our hands as caring for us, mindful of our compassionate hearts getting through this time.

- Choose a favorite dance song, turn it on, and dance. Our connection with the music and the movement touches a deep part of us, a part that counters any terror we may be experiencing.

- Write a letter to your younger self, letting them, her or him, know what you've learned about yourself while going through this.

- Write down three things a day for which you are proud. I highly recommend doing this with three things for which you're grateful. But stating the small wins you have each day reinforces the strength you're bringing to this new process.

- Let something go each day. Rather than making sure you get everything on your to-do list checked off, see if there's something that doesn't have to get done today, and let it go. Give yourself a pass. This is a great time to give ourselves a well-needed break. So, if you can let something go, even if it's skipping these exercises, it's a gift you're giving yourself.

WEEK FIVE:
When Is This Going to End?

We've hunkered down and we've stayed the course. We're tired, we're unfocused, we're cranky, and we're over it. Yet, caring for ourselves and making sure we're all well is not a one-time deal. I hate that. In all things, I prefer to go after something, get it done, appreciate what I've accomplished, and then, *Bam*, I can go on to the next thing. Take cleaning. It's been a great distraction to clean. My office is sparkling. My closets are in order. Yet, when I was dressing this morning, I saw that things were not exactly the way they were when I refolded and cleared out my drawers on Friday. And when I got to my office today, I could see dust accumulating again. Cleaning can be great, but it's a never-ending job. And that's pretty much how it feels to move on with life during the Coronavirus.

I didn't think it would be easy to cancel all my plans, work remotely, and live in a small apartment with my family, each of us with our own style of being. Nor did I know that who I thought I was prior to the Coronavirus needed an update during social distancing. I am more defensive, and less productive than I imagined I'd be at the start of this. I have to dredge up self-compassion from well below the self-criticism that has become the proverbial inner chatter. I need more sleep. I'm reading less. I'm deleting emails with recommendations on best practices now. There's too much to read, watch, and engage in.

My impatience, and, I imagine, the impatience of so many of us to "get on with our lives," is a disruptive hum as we go on with life as we've come to know it. This is a process fraught with uncertainty. Our minds like definitive answers, and there are none now. It is challenging to stay in the moment, living for the now. And we've come to understand that the only thing we are certain of is the uncertainty.

Unconsciously, to combat the uncertainty, I've been hard on myself. It's an old habit that comes out when things get tough. We all have old behaviors that sneak up on us when we're stressed. Some of those behaviors have taken hold as we march on in quarantine. My challenge is to name it and then bring compassion, patience, and loving understanding to myself, even as my thoughts veer to benign cruelty. I don't like that I'm mean. So, I'm working to do better. It is an on-again-off-again process.

Though I'm not 100% grateful for this, one of the gifts of this prolonged social distancing is that we can work on self-care in a way we might have missed out on before. My moods and negativity are now front and center. Making incremental changes that will help me to live life with more consideration, and more care is a priority at this time. And, as the announcements come in prolonging social distancing, I am given more time to employ compassion moment by moment, day by day.

Self-Care Tips:

- Stretching – It allows me to feel my body, but it's gentle. Sometimes I add sound, like a Sigh, a groan, or an Ahhh to it, for a more substantial release.

- Taking a Moment – I walk away from whatever I'm doing. This helps to see something from another vantage point. It allows me to look at something differently, and in this new view, my mind shifts.

- Breathe – I know, I know, it's so pedestrian. And, yet, focusing on our breath, whether we choose focused breathing or some other form or discipline, gives us a pause and creates a bridge to a calmer moment.

- Drink a glass of water – Getting the water and drinking it gives us a chance to recalibrate. Not only do we hydrate, but we take ourselves out of the negative moment into something more neutral.

- Turn on a Song and Dance – Moving changes everything. I might cry or smile so big. It's a mood changer like no other.

Endurance During the Coronavirus

In New York, we were told this weekend that we will continue to social distance until May 31st, at which time they will reassess. We're in this for the long haul. It is redefining the way we care for one another, the way we grieve, and the manner in which we hope.

This past week, the sadness of the many losses and the buzz of shared anxiety took its toll. I make regular mistakes, but this past week my mind was mush, and the mistakes and forgetfulness hit a new high. Or is it a new low?

We are all doing our best to adjust to continued uncertainty. But it's wearing on us. I zig right to maintain social distancing on one side, while a young couple side-by-side almost touch me as they stroll past me to my right. I watched an SUV pull out of a spot today, scraping the car behind and zooming off while the driver was looking at me looking at her. It bothered me much more than witnessing something like that in the past. Gone is my calm resolve.

I notice I'm zoned out when I need to be resting. My ability to soothe myself is limited. Years of yoga and meditation seem like memories, even as I practice daily at home or in my office. There is wear and tear to living through this pandemic. I can feel it in my achy limbs.

And, yet, I also know it may have been a hard weekend, a bad morning, but it will pass. There are moments of grace time and time again. So many are inspiring us with their generosity and goodwill. So many are risking their lives to provide the rest of us with so much more than I could ever have hoped for at a time like this in our history. The 7 PM cheering brings me to tears as I share in the celebration of our essential workers. Even stopping to write this allows me to release my stress and appreciate you for reading this. So, thank you for making a difference to me. I needed it today as we enter our sixth week of Social Distancing.

We will endure together in spirit, one small step at a time. Be safe. And may you stay well and/or heal well.

Self-Care Tips:

- Ask for help. Yes, we are isolated to a point, but asking for help means we are open to connecting.

- Put it into words. Writing, journaling, or recording our thoughts takes it out of our heads, giving us the ability to see how finite our upset is.

- Self-hugs or rubbing your hand or parts of your body to soothe yourself may not be a substitute for human touch from another, but it is a kindness we can give to ourselves.

- Change up your routine. Sometimes, something as simple as walking on a different block or washing your hands in the kitchen rather than the bathroom can shift the way we see things.

23

WEEK SEVEN:
Death During the Pandemic

We hear the numbers daily. Yesterday, the number of those on record who have contracted the Coronavirus in the US was 991,000. And the death toll yesterday was close to 1,200. My father, Irving Dubin, was one of the near 1,200 yesterday. And he is now one of the 1,537 recorded deaths in Pennsylvania thus far. But numbers tell very little about the specific lives impacted from by the Coronavirus.

Dealing with death while at the same time making adjustments for staying safe during this pandemic is not a fine balance. It's more like falling again and again and getting up each time, bruises and all. It's a strange time to be grieving. It's a surreal experience in the best of times. At least that's my experience. Under these conditions, we don't have the norms in place that we can fall back on for traditional support.

On the one hand, I appreciate the solitude afforded me at this time to privately contemplate the life my father led. He, like us all, was a man of contrasts. At times, he was enormously generous; at other times he was frugal when it didn't make sense to me. He was caring and kind and also unaware of exactly what his children did for a living. We will miss the laughs, and even the more frustrating moments. I am acutely aware of the luxury of getting angry at those we love. The hope is that we get the opportunity to work through those feelings. Luckily, his children had the chance to do that.

Some people impose their feelings about the Coronavirus and the choices we make in our mourning process. As of today, we have no plans for a Zoom service or Shiva. I love that it's available for those who want it. It's been a lifeline for thousands. But my parents' kids value our privacy. Funny I should write that as I put out this blog. The irony is not lost on me.

Yesterday was an appropriately rainy day. Really, it felt like a gift. I was able to go for a long walk through empty streets and Central Park. I imagined it would help me clear my head, which was such a jumble of thoughts and feelings. Luckily, I didn't have to fret about others getting too close since I barely saw anyone else. I was able to spend the time thinking of my dad, and thinking of friends and family. There is something so soothing about walking in the rain. That's something I would not have been able to do had I set my mind to making arrangements to do more.

We will plan for something in the future. At least that's what we've said to one another. How everything plays out is too soon to tell.

Like my father, I am filled with contradictions. The social side of me found great comfort and support thanks to social media. So many people reached out with kind words, charitable donations, and thoughtful memories. I am moved beyond words. While I was indoors during the heavy rains, Facebook kept feeding my sister, my sister-in-law, and me touching messages.

What a gift it was to spend the day of my father's death inside and outdoors while it rained and rained. Tears and rainfall in our shared grief.

Self-Care Tips for those in grief:

- Say no if you like. This is the time to do less if that works best for you. It is the perfect time to withdraw into ourselves when we need space.

- Say yes when it sounds good to you. Sometimes, sharing pleasures or hard feelings with others is a great comfort.

- Ask for help. People want to be helpful, and if we ask with an open heart, we are more likely to get something we need.

- Assume the best in others. We are all going through this difficult time, and everyone is doing the best they can. It's easy to get upset or defensive when we don't feel heard. But it happens, and perhaps we can appreciate if there is willingness. Find out the intention. Usually things are done with a positive intent.

There's Nothing Normal About This

My frustration is showing up in a myriad of ways. This morning I found out my schedule changed for the week. This is after asking others to alter their schedules. I was furious. My anger is not specifically about the schedule shift. At other times I would have been frustrated, perhaps, or mildly annoyed. But simple things are getting to me, and the steam is rising at an accelerated rate. Picture a cartoon character with puffs of smoke coming out of the ears, and you have an animated picture of too many moments of living through a pandemic.

But it's not just the heightened aggravations. Yesterday I spent my day off doing paperwork for my practice. On a good day, it can take a couple of hours at most. But after four hours of addition, correspondences, and forms filled out, I still hadn't finished. It's not as if there's a lot more to do than at the beginning of the year. But my ability to focus is highly compromised. I'm forgetting easily, getting things wrong, and spacing out.

I tried making a nice meal this weekend. I was a grouch in the kitchen. Asked if they could help, I told my family to "leave me alone." It wasn't a difficult meal, but it wasn't a known recipe. So, I tried to focus on the simple tasks even as I fumed that I was making it. No one was insisting on the meal. But we had the ingredients, and damn it, I wasn't going to waste them. In the past, cooking has been more of a pleasure. I see so many accomplish great things on their social media pages, but I am less inclined to prepare food now, burnt out from the daily business of living through this.

We all know the changes we've been experiencing these last couple of months. We're irritable, our patience is being tried, we are fearful, and we are sad. We get angry at those who handle life differently at this time through the Coronavirus. We are exhausted, depleted, and trying all manners of self-help. Some of us can't read, need hugs we can't get, and need to laugh even as our humor has diminished.

So much is amiss.

As I have written in the past, I love walking. For years it felt like meditation in motion. Since the social distancing orders, walking can be a dangerous business. Like every-one I've heard, I, too, enjoy it when the sun is out and the temperature is warm. It truly brightens my day. But, if I try to go for a long walk any time after 8 AM, I am fraught with anxiety as I weave in and out of folks without masks, or who take up the lion's share of the sidewalk. In the past, pre-COVID-19, there was a freedom we all shared. Most of us could make choices about where we went or who we saw. We could stop to talk to neighbors or hurry along so we wouldn't have to listen to others. Those choices are not available to us in the same way now.

Sometimes, we just need to complain, even as we understand that so many throughout our country, and the world, are suffering in unendurable ways. We are not condemned, but we are impacted. I am stopping to express my upset, but I also have to move forward after that. It takes more stamina these days to rally past the frustration and angst. I doubled my meditation, but the two twenty-minute breaks per day are not nearly enough to face off the shared anxiety so many of us are experiencing. I no longer watch the news on the Coronavirus. I prefer reading about it briefly to hear the latest. It helps to remember the things that we accomplished for which we are proud. Sometimes, I am simply proud to have gotten through the day.

So, here we are. In the middle of trying to figure this out, attempting to move forward as we stay in place. I am no model for getting through this. Listening to others, I'm more the norm, of feeling lots of strong feelings and appreciating the sweet moments in between. I guess that's the only normal we have. This is hard, and we all can feel that.

Self-Care Tips:

- March (if you're able) in your apartment, home, basement, or outside. With each step, stamp out frustration or agitation.

- Stroke the skin on your body. The stroking is a soothing action that can be helpful to calm us. If you can keep the strokes soft and gentle, that helps.

- Watch silly videos or anything that will make you laugh. It's such a great release.

- If you find you are being critical of yourself, see if you can use it as information on how difficult this is. Often, we criticize ourselves as a way of managing hard feelings. Just see if understanding that allows for some kindness and patience to come through.

- Subtract something from your day. Purposely don't do at least one thing. We need breaks, and we can give them to ourselves.

Glimpses of Grace in the Time of Coronavirus

It's been way too easy to name what we miss. I miss the illusion of making set plans. I miss getting about the city freely. Traveling where I like. I miss smiling to strangers and receiving one in return. And, of course, the list goes on for all of us. On the other hand, it's effortless to complain these days. The grievances come tripping off the tongue with no struggle at all. Perhaps I should thank the maskless and the rule breakers of social distancing for giving me such straightforward targets for my angst. Your non-compliance is nothing if not anxiety-producing, not to mention dangerous, so when you come too close, you are leaving yourself open for my unedited directives. "Wear a mask." "Six feet, please." "Hey, I'm walking here!"

Nonetheless, reminiscent of a natural wonder are those

moments of joy that are like a breath of fresh air under our face masks.

We're all impacted, even though some of us are medically vulnerable. Loneliness takes so many forms now.

Self-Help Tips:

- Cry. Find music, a commercial, or a show that will help you cry. Crying is a great release.

- Move slowly. We're used to rushing, but moving slowly helps us connect to our bodies in a caring way.

- Rediscover art, books, crafts, or anything creative in your home. I easily forget to really look at the paintings in my home and office, but when I see them anew, it's delightful.

- Talk out loud. Whether you record it, speak to someone else, or just say your thoughts aloud, it helps to hear them rather than keep them stuck in your mind.

A Walk in the Woods

This weekend, I went on a hike in the North Woods of Central Park. It was warm. And, yet, it was empty in the North Woods, unlike more popular areas. I was able to move freely up and down hills, trekking on dirt paths. It was heaven. This is the park I've loved all these years, a necessary sanctuary in the middle of Manhattan. I've missed being able to move freely since we became aware of Coronavirus cases in the city. As much as I love walking, traditionally finding it imperative for my well-being, moving on foot with a sense of danger lowers the level of pleasure I derive. So, spending the afternoon rambling past birds, and dense greenery, was a gift that restored my spirit.

I have spent the last two and a half months, like so

many, navigating an emotional minefield. Angry outbreaks shocked me, as I thought I was fine until I lashed out. Mostly, I've felt overwhelmed. To quell these feelings, I've been fortunate enough to work with courageous individuals who inspire me. I also meditate, talk through my issues, and find humor where I can. And I practice self-compassion, again and again, because I am behaving in ways that lend themselves to double down on patience and kind-heartedness. I am eating delicious foods, often with abandon. Sometimes I'm simply eating to medicate. I have a cocktail in the evenings, enjoying the fuzzy feeling it produces. Before COVID-19, cocktails were for parties and gatherings with friends. I am judgmental of myself. Our apartment tends to be chaotic, yet I don't have the energy nor the inclination to clean it every day. I'm critical of Larry, my husband, and Alex, my son, even though they've been helpful in so many ways. I don't compliment or thank them enough, but apparently, I can't point out perceived deficits enough, either. These are not qualities I'm happy to share, yet admitting my flaws can help to lessen their potency. It makes room for kindness and patience with myself, as well as with my family. I'm finding that ongoing compassion is essential to muddling through the pandemic.

That's why the North Woods was so soothing. I was alone in a rare patch of New York City nature, joyful and rejuvenated. The experience, along with a bike ride and a walk during the weekend, gave me the impetus to be kinder to myself and my family. On my bike ride, I passed the North Woods while a light wind gently glided past my masked face. I watched dog owners in fields keeping their social distance as their pets frolicked in the grass. These rare but essential experiences bring me back to a peaceful place of gratitude.

When I get home I am more accepting. I can laugh with Larry and Alex with ease. They are good company when

I'm centered. Though being centered has been challenging these days. Nonetheless, I will take the gifts where I can. I am thankful that the city has kept the parks open. And on those days I can't stay in the parks when they're crowded, I will always admire a tree or the flowers. And, in the hours that I can roam freely in the park, even if I have to walk a couple of miles to reach a quiet corner, I will continue to take it in. Food for my soul.

Self-Care Tips:

- Stop to smell the roses. Sometimes we pass beautiful nature too quickly. Especially in the city, when nature is spotty, stopping to admire the colors and, when applicable, the scent, we get a sliver of joy.

- Ask for help. We don't have to do this alone. Reaching out to friends or those you trust can be just the support you need.

- Sing aloud. In the shower, in your bedroom or wherever, singing alters our energy.

- Compassion, compassion, compassion. We need it for ourselves, and others need it too. When we are being hard on ourselves, pull out the compassion card and see if it can soothe.

- Find nature if you're able. If you're quarantined, do you have plants, or a window that looks out on a tree? If you are social distancing, are you able to walk on the grass, walk on the beach, or go into the woods? If so, enjoy.

Ambivalence with Mindfulness

We keep hearing how mindfulness is the way to go. It brings us back to the now. But I'm not loving the now so much. This is my struggle to use mindfulness techniques with my tendency to deny what I don't like.

I have started this blog twice this weekend already. I was feeling grateful that Larry learned how to shuck oysters, and we could enjoy them now at home. I was grateful that I have a comfortable bed for a much-needed, yet rare, nap in the afternoon. I was grateful for all the workers who make life bearable during the Coronavirus. It felt so good to then be open to the writing process. After one paragraph, I stopped. There were work issues, home chores, and unanswered texts and calls to make. I got busy. The business kept me from enjoying my bounty. It took me far away from blissful gratitude.

The weekend continued, and I continued to do my meditations, mindful-ish walks, stretching, taking photographs, or making tentative plans with Alex and Larry. I found comfort in each, at the time. But then my mind would whirl with have-tos and shouldn'ts. My brain was spinning with all the things I wanted to change as soon as I could get to them. The apartment, though small, harkens with projects to be done. The bathroom ceiling is caving in from a leak that's been "fixed" numerous times over the years. We don't want someone to come into our space, but we don't want the ceiling to fall on us either. Lucy, a joy, needs daily walks. Once out, it's a pleasure to go at her sniffy pace, but I get annoyed that I have to take her out in the middle of some project or other. Fixating on these and other moments seems like the opposite of mindfulness.

Sheryl Crow Sings, "It's not having what you want, it's wanting what you got." Great sentiment, but really? Yes, I have enjoyed having less to do so I can recover from the stresses of living and working in a pandemic. Yes, it's nice to appreciate some quality time with Larry and Alex. However, the reality is that we are usually in our own corners of the apartment during our waking hours. Most of the time, however, I'm not enjoying this moment. Most of the time, I'm not thrilled with my impatience, ire, sadness, or existential loneliness. Most of the time, it's not quality time; it's enduring this phase and getting through it.

Nonetheless, I will continue to practice mindfulness. I will practice eating slower and enjoying the experience. A practice that I often forget to employ. I will continue to meditate, often enjoying the idea of it, if not the actual practice of meditation. I will work on walking mindfully, even if that means I experience righteous indignation at those who fail to wear a mask or move away so we can safely pass. I had imagined that mindfulness was a way to a more joyful life. A promise to erase fear, grief, loss, anger, and other uncomfortable feelings. But during the time of the Coronavirus, I see that it is simply a time to be. I actually feel uncomfortable feelings more, not less. And, if I'm telling the truth, I'm not completely grateful for all these difficult emotions. But here I am, my ambivalent self, like the rest of us, sheltering in place at this moment in history.

Self-Care Tips:

- Draw or Paint. If you enjoy it, great. If not, see if you can remember being a child, and draw or paint with abandon, relishing the process rather than the result.

- Try a new food or spice. Just taking in a new experience with your sense of taste can open other areas of your mind.

- Clean out one drawer, shelf, or corner of your home. We might not be able to do the big projects, but tackling something small can give us a sense of accomplishment.

- Light a candle, if it's safe. A flame can be a symbol of transmutation.

WEEK TWELVE:
Being & Doing

Before I present my blog, I felt it important to state the obvious. These past weeks have been a floodshed of events that highlight the fatal risks that black people face when going about their lives. I am not the right spokesperson for that. There are excellent links. These are a couple I know, but there are so many sources to check to see how we can learn. My job as a white person is to stop and listen.

I suggest going to YouTube and listening to Trevor Noah speaking about George Floyd and US racism. Another wonderful site is The Free People Project.

I tend to keep myself busy. But now that we're in a pandemic and I'm older, I'm exhausted much of the time. Do I rest, or do I push through to get things done? And there's so much to do. I'm not making bread, so that's one thing I can take off my list. Though pictures of bread look beautiful on Instagram, yeast and I have a dubious relationship, and I'm not inclined to revisit it any time soon.

Nonetheless, cleaning is a necessary chore, even if I can only handle the bare minimum. I have a full practice, which takes time and attention. I take walks, go for runs, ride my bike, and do small workouts to release tension and give my body a break from sitting. Meditation takes time, too. Plus, there's cooking and reading, spending time with my family, and walking Lucy. What about resting? What about being in the moment?

For me, making a distinction between busyness and productivity is essential. Am I working hard so I don't have to face something? Am I busy so that I can avoid feeling an unpleasant emotion? Or do I feel accomplished in what I'm doing? Can I be present while being active? These are the questions I ask myself as I run around both in and out of the moment.

I kept up a relentless pace at the beginning of the quarantine, certain that was my obligation. And, when I burnt out, when I had no more to give, I'd collapse each day, unable to chat with friends, so weary was I. There's a distinction between exhaustion and rest. When exhausted, I find that the circumstances force me to halt. When I rest, I have a conscious say in my well-being. So, I am now resting more. My days off feel like days off. I might get a little done, but my to-do list is predominantly at a standstill.

No longer am I justifying being busy by taking meditation breaks. Devoting twenty to thirty minutes to meditating is not a fair balance of spending the rest of the day going non-stop. Sheltering in place continues to put a magnifying glass on pre-existing issues. It's been a time in which the volume is turned up. It will take me more time and space to learn when to succumb to rest and when to accomplish a goal. Having more bandwidth for my own uncertainty will allow me to listen to my intuition. And my intuition will guide me to make the best choice at that moment. So, let's give ourselves a break, literally and figuratively, as we continue to live in the time of the novel Coronavirus.

Self-Care Tips:

- Lower your voice. Our emotions are heightened now, and with that, our voices increase. Do what you can to soften your voice and tone. Doing that simple act helps to decrease agitation and calms us down.

- Listen. We tend to be reactive at this time. If we can stop ourselves and just listen to what we are hearing, we will find a connection.

- Donate. Giving to someone or something outside ourselves is a gift for the giver and receiver. If you don't have time to give, donate money. If you don't have money, give your time. If you have neither, give a helping hand to a neighbor or family member. Or just be a sympathetic ear. Giving to another is a way of taking us out of our busy minds.

- Look in the mirror. Smile at yourself and tell yourself that you matter. It is not about judging yourself and looking for flaws or changes, but to really see your eyes looking back at you and sending caring thoughts. Give yourself that love.

- Take a moment, breathe, sigh, and assess where you are and what you might need.

WEEK THIRTEEN:
An Air of Change

The parks, plants therein, city flowers and trees have provided a level of calm in a highly anxious time. When our metropolis necessarily closed businesses and art institutions for the greater good, living in tight quarters with few distractions has felt stifling, to say the least. Even looking for moments in nature have been disrupted by those without masks who haven't honored social distancing. It took a good month to find empty paths and safe havens for slices of calm in the ongoing stress of this pandemic.

Thanks to a recommendation, I took a long walk on Riverside Drive yesterday. I slowly ran through Central Park, taking the bridle path and dirt trails along the way until I hit Central Park North. From there I headed west to Riverside Drive. It was so quiet, much like the summers before we ever heard of COVID-19. There was a continuous balcony of greens offering much-needed restoration. The aroma of a verdant spring was in the air. It was exactly what I required before starting yet another week in the pandemic epicenter.

I even hugged a tree. It felt nice to share my appreciation with one of the many trees I encountered. I didn't care if anyone saw me. And, though the road was clear for most of the time, there was a family playing close by when I went in for the hug. It's so freeing to be at an age when I just don't care if they thought I was crazy. Crazy Coronavirus times call for crazy acts of self-care. And we all need care now. There is much repair to be done. Compassion and kindness are radical acts only if they aren't limited to only those who think similarly. Let's care for ourselves, especially when we've been hard on ourselves for all the things we have and haven't done. Let's be considerate to others, especially those who are telling us they have been oppressed and have faced ongoing deprivation and discrimination.

Let's disrupt the status quo with love, care, compassion and respect. Let's heal all that ails us.

Self-Care Tips:

- Hug a tree. Whether you do that literally, or whether you just enjoy the company of a tree near you, the strength of the roots feeding the power of the giant plant is a positive metaphor for what many of us need.

- Find your sense of humor. There is a time and place for laughter, but finding levity, even in extreme times, allows for emotional resilience when we need it most. Look at old TV shows you enjoyed, page through *The New Yorker* for the cartoons, and find the absurdity in forgetting the many things that elude us when in Corona brain.

- Get a coloring book or a paint-by-numbers kit if you need an experience of control. Though it has its limits, being able to color within the lines during the Coronavirus, a time that challenges our sense of order, provides a concrete project in mental equilibrium.

- Paint on a Zen Board. It is the art of impermanence. Simply dip the brush in water and paint on the board. You can see your artwork and it fades to a blank canvas. It helps to remind us that social distancing will pass, and we can start over again.

- Give of yourself. In a time when there are so many avenues to stand up against racism, we are given an important opportunity to donate our money, time and talents so we can advance the anti-racist movement forward.

WEEK FOURTEEN:
How am I?

How are you? Now more than ever, it's a loaded question. How many of us feel fine these days? How do we answer the question honestly?

When I hear from someone or pass an acquaintance who I barely recognize while wearing a mask, I get the question, "How are you?" Before the Coronavirus, I would say, "Fine." Fine was a quick and concise answer to a vague question. However, these days the query seems so fraught. I can honestly answer, "Fine," meaning I have not contracted COVID-19 as of today. But have any of us really been fine through the pandemic?

This weekend, I was walking down First Avenue on my way to a health food store. It was a destination walk, clocking around two miles. I like seeking out destinations. It perpetuates the illusion that I know where I'm going. In this case, I was picking up peaches. One of the few pleasures of Spring 2020 is delicious, fresh fruits and vegetables. I'm grateful for the farmer's markets and stores that provide us with these agricultural delicacies.

Step after step, imagining I was fine, I strode on a sunny day on the shady side of the street to stay cool. Suddenly, a couple barrels out of a Dunkin Donuts with their masks down, ready to sip their iced teas. Without thinking, I say, "Hey, I'm right here," a startled reaction indicating their lack of social distancing. And the woman responds with deep disdain, "Oh, shut up!" Well, that just did it. I felt like an indignant thirteen-year-old when I said, "F&*%k you." I kept walking even as I yearned to look back. Even in my frustrated ire, I remembered that a good exit means not turning around to peek. Yet I also knew at that moment my "fine" façade was a thin veneer of acceptability, easily pierced with the slightest provocation.

As I continued south, I thought of that woman. I'm sure she was having a hard time of it, too. Even so, when our paths crossed too close for my comfort, I was not in a charitable mindset. I found her petty and nasty. Not okay. And I was petty and nasty, too. I guess we were well-matched at that moment. Each of us unloading our pent-up frustrations.

I wonder if having unburdened myself of some negativity allowed me to enjoy my evening with Larry and Alex. Maybe releasing the emotional valve provided a reset.

So, if I say, "I'm okay" or "I'm fine," what I'm really saying is, "I'm adequate given the extenuating circumstances." But I'm not completely fine, as in, I have not been my best self. So, I'm using this time of continued social distancing, along with the Black Lives Matter movement, to learn and grow. Perhaps I can find healthier ways to release my anger. Then I will indulge in a fresh peach, eliciting joy in the midst of the stressful pandemic.

Self-Care Tips:

- Forgive ourselves. We may find that our tempers are short, or we're not as restrained as we'd like. Let's give ourselves some room for these missteps. Apologize when appropriate, but also make sure we can comfort ourselves since the outbursts might be an indication that we're less than okay.

- Enjoy seasonal foods and beverages. Taste is a gift. Utilize that particular sense to derive pleasure this Spring.

- Stretch. Sitting for long periods of time tightens our muscles. Stretching is a great way to soothe our bodies and clear our minds.

- Keep a gratitude journal. Writing down three things for which we're grateful each day helps us cultivate feelings of satisfaction.

- Make yourself comfortable. Check in with yourself to see if you need to stand, sit elsewhere, find a new pillow, or find a different position that brings comfort at a time when you're dealing with uncomfortable topics.

WEEK FIFTEEN:
Diminished Choices

Summer is here. But it's not like summers of our past. Vacation options are restricted. Outdoor dining is limited. And sometimes the choices at hand are not terrific. So, what to do? If I can't make long-term plans, I can think of what may or may not take place on any given day.

Take this morning, for instance. My plan was to walk to Central Park, take a slow run in the shadiest, least crowded spots, then come home to write this blog post. I tried writing yesterday, but I hit a wall in all things productive and rested more than anything else.

So, earlier today, I left later than planned and walked to the park, noticing the bustle of Stage 2 of our city opening. I was, in turn, impressed and apprehensive. I listened to a book, did my run, and had the pleasure of speaking with a friend ɑnd purchasing fruits for the week. Okay, okay, I may have found a good number of ways to procrastinate, but in the end, I'm sitting here thinking about the choices I made to start my day.

What I've noticed, more in retrospect than at the exact moment, is that I'm making small choices throughout each day. Most of these are seemingly insignificant decisions based on what's right in front of me. Even with the to-do lists I write, if I don't review them, it's probable that less than half the items on that list will get done. Instead, I assess my wants and needs, or I impulsively make a determination because I can. I checked out my office grocery needs by stopping into Whole Foods. I had no intention of going there this morning, but I was passing by, and it seemed like a good idea. As it turned out, it was a good idea. They had exactly what I wanted, and the store was pretty empty. I was in and out in less than fifteen minutes.

However, good choices are hard to come by these days. I'm noticing that choices during the pandemic have been informed by my perception of what will keep me and others safe. Sometimes, the choices were fraught with anxiety. Where can I walk, keeping proper social distancing? What can I say that is respectful to others while holding my personal truths? How can I maintain patience in the face of grief and stress? And, how do I let go of plans that have changed while finding joy in the everyday? I have no definitive answers. At times I'm successful in finding ways to answer them truthfully. And, sometimes, I get it wrong and have to learn from these failures to find grace under fire.

I think we're all exhausted from calibrating these small choices. But when plans can't proceed, and I'm faced with a lack of control, then I'm left with the small choices of everyday living. They aren't fancy, but, when I make them consciously, they keep me grounded. And, when I'm a bit out of it and I make a choice, I get to assess the benefits, or lack thereof, when I'm fully present again.

There will come a time when we will navigate our world

post-COVID-19. When and how remain to be seen. For now, I can choose a proper mask each day and live moment by moment, choice by incremental choice.

Self-Care Tips:

- Choose one brave act a day. Make it small. Choose to say "yes" to something that is unfamiliar. Or choose to say "no" to something that doesn't sound right.

- Write a letter from your future self. Write from a place of having accomplished something you've wanted, or having a viewpoint of something you've learned.

- Laugh. If you can't find something funny, use an old acting exercise and force yourself to laugh aloud until it turns into a genuine laugh. Sometimes it helps to do it with others, because laughter is contagious.

- If you are thinking negative thoughts, when you're alone say them to yourself out loud. But do it in an accent, not in your own voice. It allows you to hear harsh thoughts in a different way and can lessen their impact.

- Find a smooth patch of skin on yourself and rub it. It will bring tenderness to your self-care. I like the inside of my forearm. If you can't do that, find fabric that is soft and rub that to soothe yourself.

Attending to the Mundane

While social distancing and quarantining, when necessary, I have experienced, as we all have, moments in which we are faced with small but necessary tasks. Cleaning, for me, is one of those responsibilities that feels great when it's done, yet I procrastinate getting it done. This weekend I had to defrost my small office freezer. It's not so difficult as it is annoying. And, even on the annoying scale, it's pretty low, especially when we have to deal with so many annoyances while going through this COVID-19 period. Nonetheless, when the ice trays can't be removed, and my Tito's bottle is stuck, both from neglect as well as frost accumulation, it's time to take on the mini-fridge.

The nice part about it is that I can do it in stages. The first stage is to empty out everything from the refrigerator. Mostly it's water bottles, beverages, and condiments.

I place anything that needs to be kept cold in a bag. Then I turned off the unit, opened the door, and placed a large, absorbent towel in front to prevent flooding. Next, I hauled the bag one and a half blocks to where I placed it in my apartment fridge. From there, I went for a walk.

I loved the walk. It was a hot and humid day yesterday. So, I walked a bit slower into Central Park, then north on the bridle path, and uptown once again to the shady north woods along a brook. It was quiet and peaceful. I try to take paths I don't know. It's fun to get lost and see things I might not have seen before. Or find that I can see them from another vantage point. After I was satisfied and tired, I trekked back home. When I made it to the East side, it started to rain gently. Perfect. The streets empty out, yet the precipitation is light enough to barely get wet. I could smell the musky, sweet aroma of a storm to come.

I was instantaneously brought back to summers of yore when I would be playing outside and had to run in, sometimes getting my red Keds wet in the process. It was a routine perfumed scent, yet very specific, bringing joy to me as I made my way back home. Once home, I saw that the rugs needed vacuuming, and I had just enough energy to get that done. Again, a mundane task, yet I recalled all the weekends as a child I had to stay in until I finished my chores. One was to dust and vacuum the living room, a golden carpet under staid furniture that barely hosted activity.

There is much in these small moments, these mundane undertakings that recall memories. Today, I went back to my office to wipe down the refrigerator and restock it, remembering broken freezers in my twenties and impromptu parties so the goods wouldn't spoil. These mundane projects remind us that getting through this time of the Coronavirus connects our troublesome present with our past, as well as hope for a safe future. A future when we can blend banal moments with pleasurable diversions like walking in Central Park with a friend.

Self-Care Tips:

- Read poetry. There's everything from accessible poetry like Mary Oliver, Billy Collins, and Maya Angelou. Or other forms such as Rumi, Nikki Giovanni, Mark Doty, and Shakespeare. There are also really funny and fun poems if you'd like to lighten your day. Elinor Lipman on FB has very funny poems (they have a left slant). Or go basic like Dr. Suess, Shel Silverstein, or Dorothy Parker.

- Decorate a mask. Make your mask your own. Draw lips, or if you're okay getting messy, put on bling and sparkles. Enjoy presenting your creativity when out.

- Hydrate. Being outdoors in the summer can be fun, but staying hydrated allows for even more fun. If you are opposed to drinking water, find flavored, unsweetened water, or make your own. I find fresh mint leaves in my water or iced tea is really refreshing.

- Clear up one small area in your space. Whether you tackle a drawer or simply straighten up your work area by going through some papers and making it a bit tidier, it will help to bring the smallest bit of mental space.

- Be silly. Find the playful child in you.

WEEK SEVENTEEN:
On My Bike

Each one of us has been impacted by the Coronavirus in a personal way. Some have been ill. Many have been in quarantine. Too many have lost their jobs and income, and some of our loved ones have died. And, the weight of the pandemic continues. Friends have been divided based on the level of protection we have chosen. Plans have been canceled. Supply chains are interrupted. And we have all made appropriate adjustments centered on what is right for us under these circumstances.

I am riding my bicycle more than I have in past years. I like it because once I pass the trafficked streets, it's easy to ride the slow lane in the park. And, as with every activity, I wear my mask, wishing everyone would wear theirs when in public. This is a reflection of the rumble of fear right below the surface. I am as afraid to infect others as I am of contracting a life-threatening illness. As an extra precaution, I ride at times when the park is apt to be less populated. So far, so good.

My bicycle is a low-standing, folding bike. I like the truncated height because my feet can easily reach the ground. A throwback to shaky bike riding during the long summers peddling to The Haddontowne Swim Club. I keep my bicycle in my office, located on the ground floor, to avoid schlepping it up and down the stairs of our apartment building. It's nice when I can create a simple solution. Stashing my bike in the office also gets me out more. Given these times, if it's easy, it's more apt to get done.

Humidity was high this weekend. I don't mind that so much. It's pleasant to feel a light breeze cruising down the hills. Tracing the topography of Central Park, as well as the streets on the Upper East Side, is a unique experience I encounter during my rides. It's physical and mental. And a bit more challenging while wearing my mask. I even tried a cycling mask, which was hot and constricting, making it harder to ride. So, I returned to my office for the light cotton style that allows for an easier, though somewhat restrictive, air flow.

I am both challenged and contented on these rides. For one, though a cliché, the short journey on my bike is a metaphor for my ability to face difficulties and experience joy. I have to harness the energy to get up a hill. Whether I go slowly or forge ahead, I can feel my muscles in motion. My body is supporting me in moving through space. My mind is telling me I can do it. My conviction assures me I will do it. I am grateful that I am at an age where I can trust this thinking. I didn't have that ability twenty years ago. And I understand that taking on the big and small hills builds mental and physical strength so I can face them and others like them again.

Conversely, I can enjoy the flat roads and the ease of cycling at a pace that suits me. I can enjoy the light breezes of summer as I turn the pedals. Also, I get to know the streets that are open to me. When I'm short on time or just want a different ride, I make two rights to get to East End Avenue. It's partially closed to traffic, making it a great option. Cycling on East End is convenient and stress-free. Before the pandemic, I had no idea that I lived on the top of a gentle slope. I never really saw the hilly street as anything but quiet. It's a lovely way to get to know the city's surfaces. Enjoying old pleasures now is reminiscent of childhood, when every adventure was new again.

Self-Care Tips:

- Purposelessly take a break. Rather than push through, stop, meditate, or take a breath, and slow things down a beat. It's personally affirmational.

- Send a card or a letter snail-mail to someone who has been on your mind.

- Bring fresh herb plants into your home. They smell great, and you can always clip them to flavor your meals and drinks. If you already have an indoor or outdoor herb garden, perhaps adding another fragrant herb will round out the robust fragrances.

- Change up something in your routine(s). For instance, walk a different direction to get a different view. Or, if you always brush your teeth after your shower, brush them before. It will feel odd to do something slightly differently, but it changes how we see things and will allow for a new perspective.

- Smile under your mask. It's a mood changer.

Being Okay, Not Being Okay

I am in awe at the speed and dominance my emotions morph during the time of Coronavirus. I am moved to tears by the humanity I witness or hear about. Moments later, I am immersed in fury for a perceived injustice. I am in love with my child and husband for their simple kindnesses, and then I am agitated when I turn the corner to see that some arbitrary chore or other wasn't accomplished. My pettiness is astounding. My gratitude was short-lived.

As an observer, I find this fascinating. As the subject, I find it disconcerting. More and more I'm hearing similar stories of unwieldy emotional lability. By the week's end, I am exhausted. Too tired to be social or active. So, I am resting more and more. I have found resting to be restorative. Prior to COVID-19, I thought resting was an obligatory lessening of activities when I hit a wall or got sick. No longer.

I am not a closet napper these days. Now I proudly nap, understanding the need for downtime. I hadn't realized the array of my rigid beliefs until I had to set up new rules during the time of Coronavirus. All of a sudden, I am making room for my widening range of emotional connections. I have eschewed the notion that getting the most things done is a winning strategy. And I am throwing out plans right and left in favor of what works for me in the moment.

This has been a tragic time in our world's history. And, though I recognize the losses we all have had to endure, I am also grateful for the gifts of this time. The difficulties that have come our way make it impossible to go on as before. I am unable to hide my less attractive features, like my pettiness or judgments. I can see them upfront and personal. All I have to do is go for a walk to hear my thoughts; appreciating someone who raises their mask when passing while silently cursing those who are not choosing to protect me and everyone else from the spread of COVID-19.

These are knee-jerk responses. Later, I may be able to find compassion, understanding everyone is doing the best they can. But I don't always dwell there. So, I am using my ire to teach me. I'm not defending against the notion that I get angry or disparaging of myself and others. Instead, I am learning about how and when those feelings present themselves and seeing if I can have patience for myself and others as we travel this uncharted territory on our own and all together.

Self-Care Tips:

- Change the lighting to shift the mood. We get set in the way we light things. Yet, sometimes turning off a light or changing the bulb color helps to relax us. Conversely, bringing in more or altered light can provide an emotional lift.

- Expand your vocabulary. There is something singularly satisfying in learning new words. Word Genius brings new words to your email. There are also other platforms that are terrific.

- Star Gaze. If you can, go out on a clear night and gaze up at the stars. You will see infinite possibilities, which will be a lovely contrast to the limited options we presently have. If you can't go out, then check NASA's website or go to NOVA for images.

- Light a candle. It's so simple and can remind us that a small source of light brightens large spaces.

- Add fresh herbs to the inside of your mask. One mint leaf or rosemary sprig on the inner side of the mask can make all the difference. If you don't have fresh herbs, perhaps try an essential oil or a light fragrance that makes you happy.

WEEK NINETEEN:
Unexpected Gifts

I hadn't anticipated it, but yesterday was an enriching day. It started out hot and humid, and I knew that if I was going to get out, I wasn't going to be able to move at a clipped pace. I was wary of taking my bike out, believing that the park would be crowded, and I just needed something less populated. So, I ventured out on foot listening to a new book, *Speak No Evil*, by Uzodinma Iweala, a Nigerian American author. It's beautifully written and the readers are terrific.

My destination was a Cambodian restaurant, the only one in the city. I had read about it but had never visited. I saw that it was closing at the end of the month, so I used it as a destination. I would order take-out and carry our dinner home. Though I couldn't go inside, when I stepped up to pay, I viewed a stunning interior. There were Buddhist art pieces and Cambodian décor. The owner was there, and she was more than gracious. So kind and generous, offering extra side dishes and beverages. She was losing her restaurant to the pandemic and yet wanted to treat me to something extra. Her kindness softened my spirit.

Then, in the evening, I was tired but not sleepy, so I perused Amazon, Apple TV, and finally Netflix. It was there that I found an intriguing documentary, Mucho Mucho Amor. It's the story of Walter Mercado, a famous Puerto Rican star who brought joy to so many with his astrology readings. He was an amazing man, and I was moved by his humanity and fanciful lust for life.

I had to put the film on pause as I was finding out about his rise to fame. Lucy had to be walked, and I was the only one home who was awake. I was frustrated, but these things can't wait. We went out to our stoop. I wasn't sure if she just wanted to be out in the hot night air, or if she really had to go. Either way, she was on pause at the bottom of the steps. It was then that I heard a group chanting. I saw a few cyclists on their bikes leave what looked to be a rally. Then I heard peaceful chanting, "Black Lives Matter!" I realized that the weekly bicycle rally for the Black Lives Matter movement ended their ride in front of Gracie Mansion, the temporary residence of the Mayor. It's just down the block from our building.

There was such camaraderie. It was all peaceful. Cops were acting as escorts. I witnessed fellowship. And there was so much hope. I felt so fortunate to be a bystander to the positive power. Shortly thereafter, Lucy and I were up and on the move. They had all cycled away by the time Lucy completed her walk. And, then I was able to finish watching the film. I went to bed later than usual and was fully inspired.

So often during the time of Coronavirus, I have felt as if the days are long and so little gets done. But yesterday, though I did little, I was given so many gifts. They were all provided by individuals from other races and ethnic backgrounds. How rich life is when we learn and grow because we are in touch with those who are different from us.

Self-Care Tips:

- Enjoy something outside your familiar patterns. It could be a new cuisine, a virtual look at an international museum, reading a writer you don't know, or simply noticing things around you that may have slipped your gaze previously.

- Pause. When you are feeling overwhelmed, or you're about to act impulsively in a way that may not support you, take a moment. Be conscious of your breath. Take in a few things that surround you. And then reassess what you want your next action to be.

- Notice at least one thing that brought you pleasure at the end of your day. Of course, it could be more. Maybe it was a beam of light from your window that played on a surface. Or perhaps it was a chat with a friend. In this way, you double your pleasure as you think about those moments again.

- Keep it simple. These times are trying for most, so it helps to keep things simple when we can to alleviate extra stress.

- Do something from your childhood. Whether you choose to play a game of hopscotch on your sidewalk, skip down the block, or sing a childhood song, finding childhood pleasures is an easy way to bring joy.

WEEK TWENTY:
The Frustration Budget

The light breeze in the high heat and humidity of this New York summer is a simple pleasure these days. When I amble along on the sweltering sidewalks, I can feel the gentle air waves stroke my head and shoulders, lifting me up from the heaviness of the muggy day. It's a simple joy to feel the wind when it comes. It eases the countless frustrations that have set upon us during this time of the Coronavirus.

Given how easily I can be set off these days, I have come up with a made-up system. I have begun to enact a frustration budget. Living through a pandemic can wreak havoc on our nervous systems. So, I am going to assess what is a livable measure of frustration, and anything above that quotient will not be spent. I am not my best when I'm over-stressed. And, then I circle back on annoyance with my mood and behavior, thus adding to my agitation level.

At this point, I think I need to set up my budget with a low level of frustration. I am subtracting rather than adding to my to-do list. I am laughing at myself for my lack of memory, including my lack of access to common words, and forgetting seemingly simple tasks. I open my pajama drawer when I mean to retrieve socks from a parallel drawer. I am at work, and I am unable to make a point since the word "overcome" will not make itself known to my brain at that moment. Pre-pandemic, I would get annoyed with myself, and maybe even defensive. Now, deep in the storm of COVID-19, I am amused by my foibles. At least that's how it is at this hour.

The frustration budget will be a work in progress. I just thought of it this week, as I felt exhausted by the end of my day, and quickly followed it up by being less than pleasant when I came home. It was then I thought, "Why not limit what I take in that doesn't bring me joy?" And why not? I don't need to finish those articles now when I don't have the bandwidth. I can look at the New Yorker cartoons and save anything else that really interests me. I can leave the room if the TV is on a program I neither like nor care about. I can shorten my walk if I get exasperated by those who are not following the CDC recommendations. I can lengthen my meditation so that I purposely have more calm moments in my day.

I am amazed by the changes that have occurred since our world changed. Much of it is difficult. But some of it, like noticing that I can't continue building a wall of aggravations on top of displeasures, brings a sliver of mindfulness. It's a kindness that I can give myself. I imagine the daily distractions and activities in the past allowed me to ignore certain annoyances, but now they are front and center. It is time to tear down the wall one frustration at a time until I am thriving within my frustration budget.

Self-Care Tips:

- Notice what frustrates you and see if you can let go of anything on your list.

- Start a Bullet Journal. It's a creative way to track what's important to you.

- Keep a Mood Tracker so you can care for yourself no matter what you're feeling.

- Write personal affirmations and put them on post-its, then place them where you'll see them, like on the bathroom mirror, in your sock drawer, or on the calendar.

- See if you can laugh at yourself when you find you're being hard on yourself. It really shifts your mindset. If you can't laugh at yourself, maybe you can smile at the fact that it's not easy to go from frustration to humor.

WEEK TWENTY-ONE:
Boredom

It felt so nice to find expanded trails on Randall's Island yesterday. The monotony of life during the Coronavirus can be stifling. Though I walk daily, finding fresh paths and unseen sights has been challenging. And, to find them in places that are free from others is nearly impossible in the city. But I persevere as if it's a made- up game to challenge the norm.

I'm coming up with a lot of private games. Can I meditate and let my thoughts pass by, or will I go on a tangent and then find myself caught between my imagination and the present moment? Will I be able to find an isolated spot in the city and take a deep breath without my mask on because no one is around? Will I be able to employ grace in giving another the benefit of the doubt, or will I be judgmental? I am always the winner of these games. I am either humbled, understanding that I am still growing, or I was able to accomplish it in that moment, understanding that I will be playing that game again with no guarantee of the same outcome next time around.

I hear so often how bored we are. When we don't have our go-to activities, it can feel boring to face the void. There are a lot of theories about boredom. Some experts think that acting out of boredom is a way to incite problems that give us something to focus on. Others think underneath boredom is anger. Still other experts postulate that boredom connotes a lack of purpose. All are understandable while our world confronts COVID-19.

We miss getting together with friends and family. Many miss public gatherings. Others miss going out. Naturally, there's a lot we miss. The pandemic has been a time of loss. Too many have lost their lives, others their health, a great many their livelihoods, and most everyone misses a sense of safety.

The upside of boredom is the opportunity it provides for innovation. We are in a position to discover ourselves anew. We may find out things about ourselves we never recognized. For instance, I always thought of myself as an active individual. I liked being busy. Though I, along with so many psychotherapists, am busier than ever, I am resting more, making downtime a priority. Or we may find hidden corners of the city's parks that allow us to move freely. Or we find out that our value is not about what we have or what we do, but by how we live our lives. And we can only discover these personal truths by living through the boredom.

Self-Care Tips:

- Find a quarantine concert. There are so many, from Erykah Badu to Nora Jones and Norm Lewis. Billboard.com has a list. The *NY Times* has its own list. And there are so many more. Check out pages from your favorite artists or genres.

- The wonderful charity MIND has a twenty-four-hour free helpline: 800–123–3393. This is a mental health hotline for those who are experiencing depression and anxiety.

- Give someone the benefit of the doubt. Rather than expecting them to behave a certain way, see if you can open yourself up to another possibility.

- I just heard this adage: If it's hysterical, it's historical. When you're feeling something deeply, it can be a personal kindness to think of it as a way of working through something from your past that still plays a role in your emotional well-being.

- Give yourself permission to change your mind. Giving our word matters. Yet there are times when we are not up to doing what we committed to doing. You can then change your mind. More often than not, the other person will feel relieved with the canceled plans, too.

WEEK TWENTY-TWO:
Stressing About Stress

Oh Boy, another opportunity to stress. We are going away to unload stress from city living, and yet here I am stressing about going away. I've gotten used to the steady hum of anxiety just below the surface. I have yet to speak to anyone during the pandemic that hasn't acknowledged added stress. These feelings manifest themselves in many forms. For me, I have a hard time focusing, going from one task to another without completing any of them until I've come back around twice.

For the first time in years, we will be at a place where there is no WiFi or cell service. To that end, I set a deadline for myself to complete this post before we left. Last night was my made-up target. When I failed to do that, I had to search for another word rather than fail to come back to myself with some patience and understanding. Now I'm telling myself I simply did not finish this last night and am doing that now.

This also meant that my walk, run or bike ride was going to be short today. I didn't wake up early. Instead, I slept until I woke naturally and abbreviated my previous goals. Perhaps we'll settle in early enough for me to take a walk around the large property this evening. Or not. Either way, we're on an adventure. I am, in turn, excited and nervous. And I'm interested in how my stress will wane in the wooded Catskills.

Self-Care Tips:

- Do something sensual. This isn't necessarily sexual. This has to do with your five senses. Find a scent you like, make touch a sensate experience. Mold clay, taste something divine. Listen to the birds or music, or secondary sounds.

- Make up with yourself. Think of something for which you got mad at yourself. Now, let yourself know that you are your own reclaimed friend. As a friend to yourself, you may feel more inclined to treat yourself with respect and compassion.

- Learn something new. Whether you listen to someone who knows something you didn't know, or whether you look up information online on a site like lifehacker.com or zidbits.com, it's fun to learn facts, hacks, or material new to you.

- Do it differently. Like I had to shorten my run today, as well as my blog post, it can be relieving to accomplish something outside your routine.

- Get away. If you're not going anywhere, try a virtual tour on Fodor's or another travel website. Or take a new route on a walk. Or leave your home for a safe place in a new venue. All can expand your outlook.

WEEK TWENTY-THREE:
Make Plans and the Universe Laughs

I put a lot of stock into getting away. I was sure I needed a vacation, time away from work, and the city to regroup. We drove for a few hours until we found our rental home in the heart of the Western Catskills. It is breathtaking here. Having space to simply be has been a relief. Yet, I brought some old baggage with me. I'm not talking about luggage here; I'm speaking of my long-term dysfunctional beliefs and habits.

It took no time at all to enjoy the view from the front porch. The mountains and the greenery are simply verdant. The home has a winter lodge feel to it, and it was nice to be in a place with high ceilings, lofts, and space. I was off-line and on vacation. A pandemic vacation. A vacation in an unknown home rather than a destination further than our own state. I'm so grateful that we have a chance to get away. I know how fortunate I am to have a job that I love and am employed in this difficult time. I am aware of the privilege of being able to get away. Yet, I also know that my privilege does not make me immune to human foibles. This vacation gave me a chance to become more acquainted with a few of my shortcomings.

There's a lot to do when at a rental. Planning and preparing food, cleaning things to feel more comfortable, and getting to know the house, the property, and the surrounding area. We did well the first couple of days. We found hikes, trails, towns, and local provisions. I felt at ease in the mountains and woods.

I was fooled, though. My shoulders had softened. They were no longer touching my ears. They were making their way into their natural position below my neck on either side. That alone had me believe that I was relaxed, and there were no worries. But by day three, I was starting to weigh my relief at being in the country with my small disappointments with the house, the area, and the responsibilities. I didn't think about how much work it takes to be away like this. I was no longer used to preparing multiple meals each day. And I got resentful that I was doing so much work around the house. No one made me do it. But I learned to be a people pleaser, and I took on that role like it was 1990.

It wasn't until I became nasty because others were lounging during their vacation (how dare they!) that I saw that I was no longer giving to make others happy; I was sacrificing my rest because of some unknown sense of duty. It was not out of love, but rather out of a need to be appreciated. What I got was the opposite of appreciation. So, I got cranky. A killjoy during a vacation, or at any time, for that matter.

Thank goodness they're a forgiving bunch, or so it seems. I could go back to them and let them know that I appreciate them. And, so often when I give what I think I'm owed, it shifts my experience. I am now able to gaze up at the night sky to commune with the countless stars. I was able to go on a walk today and enjoy the space and freedom of seeing no one. It helped to take in the huge trees and the sky. Listening to the birds chirping and the lapping brook. Larry and I went for a couple of drives and came upon a lovely farmer's market. Everyone is friendly. Very refreshing.

And, when dinner needed to be made today, I was able to ask for help in a kinder way. Everyone pitched in, happily making for a lovely evening. Sometimes it takes a break to make a break from habits that never served us.

Self-Care Tips:

- Pay attention to difficult feelings. Let them be and they will reveal hidden truths that hold us back. Then, without judgment, continue to provide space for the discomfort. It will release itself.

- Write a letter to your future self. Choose how many years that will be: five, ten, twenty, or another number. In thinking about yourself in the future, also think about one thing you can do today that supports the future you to whom you wrote the letter. Then, in addition to writing the letter, take an action that supports your future you.

- Give yourself a second chance. If there's something that you've done or that you want to do but haven't done, rather than give up, giving yourself another opportunity to try it means there is no dead end to the issue.

- Be in touch with someone who believes in you. When we spend time, speak with, or are in the presence (even virtually) of someone who knows our value, we automatically feel empowered, and that promotes self-esteem. If you have yet to meet that person, look at someone who you admire and see if you feel inspired.

- Light a candle in the dark or turn on a small flashlight. You will see how one small light illuminates the darkness. Now, think of yourself and your actions as that light.

WEEK TWENTY-FOUR:
Inner Resources

Monday, I arrived home from a week in the country. It's great to be home in my familiar surroundings, working from my office. And, now that I'm home, I happily go to my closet for my clothes rather than reaching into a suitcase. The pastoral setting on vacation was restorative. Yet the familiarity of our apartment and the city is comforting in its own way.

Ever since we began to feel the impact of the Coronavirus by social distancing, public spaces closing, or our everyday lives being turned upside down, we've had to confront so many losses and harness our resilience to get through our days. While we used to have so much to look forward to on our time off, we've hunkered down, finding small pleasures during these stressful times. Our vacations are altered, while our time at home is unique to this unprecedented year.

We found a reprieve by going away for a week. But the true challenge is finding pleasure in the here and now. One thing I do is make my own Frappuccino at home. My coffee goes in the blender with ice, stevia, and almond milk. It's easy, and it cools down the summer mornings. Though it's a simple pleasure, I know I can start my day having given myself this small treat. Then, throughout the day, I stretch, breathe, and go for walks when on a break. Today I went to the park for a short run. I do what I can. We all do.

But what happens when we're feeling vulnerable? We may not have an effortless way to comfort ourselves. Sometimes we are left bereft of stamina, of internal reserves. Maybe we're having difficulty sleeping. Or we're too foggy-brained to attend to daily activities. Whatever makes us vulnerable can temporarily rob us of access to our inner resources. In those moments, even having patience is a stretch.

The idea that "this too shall pass" can be comforting. But we also feel the frustration of not knowing when this will end. So, we lurch forward on this crooked road. We endure the troubling times and embrace the small wins. We drink homemade frozen lattes and double down on meditation. We soothe ourselves when we can. And we comfort our friends and family because we all need support now. Because, after all, we're living through a pandemic.

Self-Care Tips:

- Send a love letter via email to yourself. For example: "Dear Janet, you are loved." Or "I matter." It's as simple as that. Of course, it can be more like a diary or journal entry. It's your email; you decide.

- Take a mindfulness walk. It can be five to ten minutes. Simply walk, feeling your body move indoors or out.

- Make a very small domestic change. It can be throwing out a kitchen tool that no longer serves you. Or it could be dusting the top of the picture frames. It's just something easy that is outside your usual routine.

- Do one thing fully focused, with no distractions. We are so used to multi-tasking without thinking. Instead, Try eating a snack, sitting down, conscious of the flavors and the sensation of chewing and swallowing. No TV on or phone in your hand. Or just focus on a phone call, listening without doing anything else.

- Save. If you feel that you're stuck, see if there is a way to crack a window on saving. Find one thing that is doable, then do it. For instance, if there is something you want, but the money just isn't there, start by saving some change, or a dollar at a time. It may take some time, but you get to create a way to obtain something you want.

WEEK TWENTY-FIVE:
Managing Expectations

I have to admit, I usually get disappointed on my birthday. I make lofty plans, and then things don't go as planned, which saddens me. Not this year. My birthday was this past week. The days leading up to my birthday were terrific. I got good news from a friend. Larry and Alex cooked beautiful meals. I was able to take a scenic bike ride on Randall's Island. Since it was humid, the weather kept people indoors. And, because I rode close to the river, there were breezes coming and going. I found work inspiring. And, I had little planned for my birthday. I was not anxious that my plans needed to turn out. I took care of myself as best I could, miscommunicating at times, or forgetting commitments I made. But I was not hard on myself. Heck, we're living through a pandemic.

And, when my birthday came, I was able to go to Central

Park for an early morning run before starting work. I was in a good mood, so I didn't tally the runners without masks. Surprisingly, I didn't feel unsafe. Then I made myself breakfast and went to work. I enjoyed my frozen latte thanks to my blender. And, when work was finished, I wrote briefly, met Larry, and we kept our dinner plans even though rain was predicted. Just in case, I was armed with a rain poncho and umbrella.

Ever since March, when COVID-19 limited New York businesses, we have eaten at home or in the garden on occasion. So, this was the first time in the pandemic we were dining out in the city. Hesitant at first, we went anyway. It was lovely. Dinner was delicious, it was a short walk home, and the rain came well after we were enjoying cake in our apartment. Thank you, Caroline's Cakes and Gold Belly. And I remain so grateful for the birthday wishes I received on social media. I'm not on the platforms often, given my schedule. Yet, the love and power of these days gives me a great appreciation for connecting with family and friends. It's a remarkable reminder of all the good out in our world.

I know I've been told that letting go is the way to go. It's a central premise of all mindfulness practices. But we cannot "do" letting go. I certainly can't. It's a state of being that comes following clinging onto beliefs too hard and for too long. Behavior that is all too familiar. I don't know why it took the Coronavirus to stop trying so hard to have things go right. But the pandemic and all that goes with it has allowed me to enjoy simple pleasures that have been deeply meaningful. Lowering my expectations this past week brought about unexpected gifts. The challenge now is to manage my expectations on keeping this up. Because holding on to letting go is a sure way to perpetuate that old, unworkable cycle. I'll let you know how it goes.

Self-Care Tips:

- Ask yourself what it would take to let go of something that isn't working for you. Just ask the question. No need to do anything yet.

- When looking in the mirror, smile at yourself. And you'll see that you're smiling back.

- Remember an act of kindness and remember how it felt to be the recipient or the giver of that act. Find an opportunity to give of yourself in an unexpected way.

- Take a walk in nature, if you can. And, if you can't, see if you can find nature in your environment.

- Use pen and paper to write a note, a journal entry, a letter, etc. See if it changes how you think and how you write.

Masked Strangers

I'm not being rude; I just don't know who you are. Though it seems ill-mannered, I rarely recognize anyone I see. While walking about, I hear my name but have no idea who is summoning me. Even after you tell me how we know each other, I have difficulty placing you. This is the dilemma of mask-wearing.

Sometimes, I recognize the voice. Yesterday, my name was called behind me. And, though I couldn't pinpoint who she was, ultimately, her voice gave her away. She's been our upstairs neighbor for about eighteen years. It's as if I have face blindness, a malady made well-known by the late, great Oliver Sacks.

I used to recognize everyone, even those who had no

clue who I was. I'm not great with names, but I remember faces, shared experiences, and my personal impressions. But now that we're wearing masks, and, for my part, I prefer you wear one than not, I can rarely identify neighbors, acquaintances, friends, and colleagues. It adds to the many moments in which I am caught without a clue during this time of the Coronavirus. My mind is not as sharp now as it was in January. Are any of us as focused or attentive as last year? From what I hear, no.

What I do recognize is a modern dance on the bridle path with the reservoir as a backdrop. A man was doing amazing moves as I slowly ran the path. And I can identify a small ballet class on the East River promenade. They were quite advanced. It was pure joy passing them by as they strongly and gracefully leaped in the wind.

I also recognize the dogs I know. They remain maskless for now. And in that way, I know the identity of the owner. I also recognize bees, butterflies, turtles, and horses. Most importantly, I can recognize smiling eyes. They say the soul can be seen in the eyes. And the beautiful creases that adorn perfect strangers are a welcomed reprieve from the stress of the pandemic. It connects us even when I don't know if I know you.

Self-Care Tips:

- Buy two masks and give one away.

- Shake things up, try a new hot sauce.

- Whatever you forget, whatever mistakes you make, whatever embarrassing moment you might have now, remind yourself you're living through a global pandemic.

- Smile at a masked stranger.

- Dance indoors or out, bringing joy to yourself and perhaps others.

WEEK TWENTY-SEVEN:
Outdoor Musings

It's such an odd experience to go for a walk and find myself, again and again, a focus of various restaurant patrons on the streets of New York. I realize they've been starved of social interactions. And people-watching has taken on a new importance. Pedestrians have become the dinner entertainment for the open tables' clientele. So, if I walk uptown or downtown on the avenues, I become a subject for diners' eyes. Conversely, I look to see how to walk around so I'm not too close while they're eating their meals mask free.

It may be that I provide much-needed amusement with my firecracker ponytail, my loose tee shirts, and my touristy fanny pack. I don't care. I'm at an age where I believe other people's opinion of me is none of my business. It gives me more head space to enjoy my daily walks.

The character of the city has taken on its own pandemic

configuration. For instance, I was so looking forward to this past Labor Day Weekend. In previous years, the city emptied out and we could roam freely, the streets void of residents. Not so last weekend. If anything, it felt more like neighbors had prematurely returned from second homes or vacation dwellings.

I love the East River Promenade. Yet, I'm not so fond of it during the pandemic. This summer, the river-facing benches are like chaise lounges at resorts; people have to get there early and stake out their territory. Should I identify a rare empty bench, I would have to race-walk to claim it as mine. And forget it when said bench is shaded.

When I'm out with Lucy, I get the distinct impression that she is confused that her park is no longer all hers. We walk to areas she loves to sniff, only to come across sun worshippers or picnickers who are located in the exact spot she wants to examine. So, we move on, trying to forge a path around these interlopers.

The city is, in turn, both emptier and more crowded. The indoor places are a quarter full at most, while outdoor spaces seem to be at capacity. This weekend brought even more people outdoors with cooler temperatures and Labor Day behind us. I'm looking forward to the future when travel is a safer option. My plan is to stay in the city as it empties out. Lucy and I will sit on a readily available bench. And, if they want, the runners by the river can enjoy Lucy's mellow aura and whatever quirky yet casual get-up I'll be sporting.

Self-Care Tips:

- Set an alarm on your daily calendar to acknowledge yourself for small accomplishments.

- These times are so difficult. Write down or share with others something for which you are proud.

- Set a timer for complaints. This way you can acknowledge all the things that you find annoying, but it's framed within limits.

- One-minute stretch breaks help you come back to yourself, physically and emotionally.

- People-watch when you're outdoors. You never know who you might find amusing.

WEEK TWENTY-EIGHT:
New Upsets

I won't lie, this past week was tough. I don't know whether the change in temperature reminded me of a mostly lost summer, or whether the continued stress of clients related to the NYC educational failings had me struggling after each day. I came home unready to relate to my small family except by means that pushed them away. Not good for any of us. And, then Friday night, as we were hopeful in celebrating the Jewish New Year, we heard the sad news of RBG's death. Like with so many, it feels like a personal loss.

As I have learned in the process of past bereavement, there are physical manifestations of loss. Saturday, I felt achy, with shallow breaths. It is not COVID-19. But it is similar to symptoms that prevail among my close female friends and family who also found a hero in Ruth Bader Ginsburg. A very human hero. While she championed gender equality, she did so within a binary model, and may not have given voice to certain minority groups within our population.

So much has been written about her. And it's hard to choose my favorite among her many admirable qualities. But given these times, given what we're going through individually and together, the trait that stands out to me presently is her respect for differences. She appreciated the ways we connected and understood that we are not all the same.

However, it's not a stance I often see these days. I am saddened at the hate and judgment I hear and read about related to opposing points of view. Honestly, it's hard to take in. Why can't I believe in women's rights, human rights, and Black Lives Matter without being seen as soft or a bleeding-heart liberal? Conversely, what is wrong with doing my part as I see fit rather than it being not enough if not done in a louder or more forceful fashion?

Normally I stay away from political subjects; unless you consider wearing a mask to protect each other from the Coronavirus political. I suppose I open myself up for criticism in stating my beliefs. Fair enough. It's time to live influenced by those who inspire us, rather than by those who activate our divisive natures. I choose to respect those who differ in their views. Nonetheless, I will not be bullied by those who don't respect my views. I am grateful to the eminent RBG for paving the way for shared appreciation of personal and political divergences. We can respect others' differences while living our own truths.

On a personal note, I will continue to pay attention to my own distress while working and living through this pandemic, learning new ways to care for myself. Forgiving of my sharp edges, while having the courage to be vulnerable, letting in imperfect support.

Self-Care Tips:

- Remind yourself of something for which you know yourself to be good. You can write it down, or simply remind yourself of this and other things that you know to be good.

- Give yourself one moment to make a choice of what you will do in the next moment.

- Use RBG as an inspiration and take an action inspired by her life's work.

- See if you can take one item off your "should" list. Not by doing it, but by crossing it off as something that no longer "should" get done.

- Do an anonymous kind act. It might be cleaning up after a family member, or it could be opening up a door for a stranger or making a donation. See if you can do it without seeking acknowledgment. What is it like that it is enough that you know you did it?

Weeds in Context

As a young girl, how I loved to blow the puff off a dandelion while I made a wish. And the bright yellow flowers were so nicely sprinkled about the lawn when I was growing up. I remember being told I shouldn't like dandelions because they were weeds. And, though I secretly enjoyed the seed-carrying wisps and the bright yellow blooms, I did not share this with lawn lovers in my neighborhood.

But in a pandemic, in a concrete jungle, flowers of any kind can brighten my walks. So, as I was spending a work break walking on the East River esplanade, I smiled when I came across some dandelions. I have a deep appreciation for dandelions in this pandemic. Seeing them is a bright spot during these difficult days. Not only do they bring me back to my childhood, but they also connect me to the present.

Dandelions remind me that the value of an experience is based on context. In the context of the Coronavirus, a flash of color is a small gift. In the context of suburban lawns of the 60s, that same weed was a scourge on mani-cured properties. Context really matters these days. When we think of caring for ourselves, and perhaps those we love, getting through a pandemic may present new pathways to our well-being. We may have hit our saturation point of plowing through. Now, we have to embrace the weeds of the past, both literal and metaphorical, as we wind our way on the twisted COVID-19 road. Where once I might have called myself lazy for taking a day to rest with so much to get done, these days, indulging in a respite is a loving act I can give to myself.

Let's bring out the weeds. Make a bouquet of them. We owe it to ourselves to enjoy the wild flowering plants in these turbulent times.

Self-Care Tips:

- Make a wish. If you're not able to wish on a dandelion puff, write your wish down and put it in a secret place where you might forget about it for a while.

- Actively listen. See if you can listen from a place of curiosity. Instead of adding what you know to the conversation, see if you can learn something new from the person speaking.

- Be willing to be wrong. We open up and grow if we are not attached to being right.

- Make one small change that leads to a larger change. That could mean taking out your yoga mat so that you might stretch someday soon, or it could mean you open up a new document so that you can write something you've been meaning to write. Or you buy an ingredient for a recipe you've been wanting to try.

- Whether you need inspiration or a short break, go to YouTube and search for someone who makes you smile and watch a brief video of their words, song, dance, or other offerings.

WEEK THIRTY:
Autumn is Here

This Autumn is like no other. And, given that fact, we will go through it differently than in the past. For most of us, it feels quite disorienting. We like to be able to count on what we've known to be true.

For so many of us, the Fall is when we start anew. We count on the school year, even years after we've attended school, to pace ourselves. I feel like I have to create a new pace for living through a pandemic. No one I know counted on it lasting this long. We made mental deals with ourselves to get through the first three months. And, as we enter our eighth month, we are bedraggled. At least I am.

Last week my walks were slower, and my runs shorter. I just didn't have it in me to move around the city with alacrity. Now that we're in the last quarter of the year, I am thinking about how to enjoy this period, while securing more downtime so that I can enjoy the weather, the fall colors, and moments of grace when they come. Luckily, it's beautiful in New York City. There are hints of changing hues in the parks and a clear, crisp air that propels my movements outside. But when home, I'm depleted, though I have work and life responsibilities that call.

To face this time in life, I am making the distinction, or at least I'm working on making distinctions, between the things I can and cannot control. I can wear a mask. And, when I forget to put it on, because… COVID-brain, I have an extra one in my bag that I can pull out. I can go to bed early. I can take walks. I cannot control how the day goes. And I am not always able to control my reactions. Afterward, I am able to take responsibility for those outbursts. I do apologize. And sometimes I even learn from those difficult interactions. And, when I'm being hard on myself, I can recognize that something is amiss. I then slow down to look and see what the genuine issue might be. If there is a silver lining during this pandemic, it's having the space to slow down. It might not have been a welcomed gift at first, but with time I am able to appreciate its power.

Self-Care Tips:

- Allay insomnia by writing down a list of worries that swim around in your mind. In writing them down, they can be transferred from your mind to the paper, allowing you to pick them up in the morning if you're so inclined.

- Open up your spices and sniff them. Having your sense of smell ignited expands possibilities.

- Go online window shopping. Though we might not be able to visit all the stores we like, we can take our imagination online. This way you can

look without overspending. Window shop without spending a dime. Or, if you feel you can't
look without buying, give yourself a budget so
you can choose within your financial means.

- Put an ice pack on your forehead or the back of
  your neck. The cooling sensation soothes us as
  it shifts our stressed-out feelings from tightness
  to some release.

- Give yourself a moment to slow down. See how
  that feels. Notice what you like about giving
  yourself a moment. And notice if you think you're
  giving something up by creating a moment just
  for you.

WEEK THIRTY-ONE:
Who Cares About Rewards?

I keep receiving emails warning me that my hotel or travel awards are going to expire. Or I'm enticed to go out to eat to get points and rewards. I simply don't care. In the past, I played the game and accrued points and rewards. I was happy to join one program or another to earn gift certificates for shopping, extra discounts, free meals, or nights at hotels. None of this is of interest now. The notices remind me that I have been an avid consumer, through and through.

Once in a while, I was able to enjoy a free meal or a room upgrade. Or I planned a trip in which I used miles. Mostly, though, I found myself happy to have the points or rewards while having no good use for them except in my mind. Not being able to travel during the pandemic, and mostly not choosing to eat out in the city, I am left with these impractical accounts.

These days I'm unloading rather than amassing. I go through old spices, clothes that are uncomfortable, papers that are out of date, and any number of other items that no longer serve me. I'm not sure what I'll do with my travel rewards. But one thing seems certain, continuing with most of these programs appears to be pointless.

Self-Care Tips:

- Follow Duchess Goldblatt on Twitter. It's fun, literary, and caring.

- Do a duet in the shower with your favorite solo singer. Choose your bedroom or any place you like. Use Spotify, Apple Music, Amazon Music, a recording, or track, then sing at the top of your lungs.

- Squash is in season. Branch out with a new variety like Delicata, Banana Squash, or Kabocha.

- Identify and focus your energy and attention on your strengths. This alone can support moving forward.

- Take a peek through a window into your unconscious. Keep a notebook and pencil next to your bed. Write down any images or a dream you had as soon as you wake up.

I Was Wrong

Last week I made acorn squash with essence of orange and maple syrup. I asked Larry to bring a spoon, as I thought that might be easier than a fork. He proudly came back with a grapefruit spoon. Silently, I was annoyed. Didn't I just ask him for a spoon? A regular spoon? I begrudgingly took it from him. I was tired and rather than open up with vulnerability, I found myself closing down with negativity. When I tried the spoon, which has unobtrusive serrating, it turned out to be an excellent choice for the squash. Larry likes to find the perfect tool for the job, and I was wrong to not trust him. In the past, I wouldn't have even tried the utensil. I would have marched into the kitchen to get a regular spoon. Yes, I have been known to be that petty. Yet, in this instance, being open allowed for a better culinary experience.

For years, as a defense mechanism, I have needed to be right. I would even sacrifice a better experience than admit I was wrong. Or, I'd say I was wrong but secretly think I was right. It's hard to become a better person when I can't be open to all that is unknown. There's nothing like a pandemic to test the limitations of being right. So many of us thought this would be a short stint of sacrifice followed by triumph. It is anything but that.

I am faced with my foibles as I go through my days in a pandemic. For those of us who are parents, we see the cracks in our seemingly strong facades on a regular basis. As a therapist, I'm faced with the benefits and constraints of talk therapy. We have no answers now. We can talk about and work on making changes in how we deal with our current circumstances, but we cannot immediately change the national and global ills. Personally and professionally, I believe speaking about our hardships with the intention of growing is invaluable. If you prefer something more active, vote. Also, we can deliberately make changes to the seemingly mundane. We just have to be open to doing something differently. Perhaps we'll get it right if we admit we were wrong. It's working for me. Thank you, Larry.

Self-Care Tips:

- Try using a grapefruit spoon for grapefruits, squash, and anything else you deem applicable.

- Find a course or article online on art, music, dance, or theater history. It's great to dig a little deeper into an art form you appreciate.

- Change the way you put on your shoes or other daily habits. If you're a sock, shoe, sock shoe person, put both socks on first. If you always start with your right foot, start with your left. See how it feels to switch up an ingrained habit.

- If you are incorrect about something, see if you can admit to being wrong. It might feel like a lovely release.

- Do what you can. These can be challenging times; do what you can, appreciating you're doing your best under the circumstances.

Dropping, Spilling & Breaking

Today while making chili, beans spread out in the sink while I was draining them. Usually, I'm not so lucky to have a contained spatter. Just two weeks ago, glass shattered in all directions. I put on my shoes and cleaned up the shards that extended into two rooms. I've certainly seen an uptick in drops, breakages, and absent-mindedness. It seems to have increased in these last few weeks. Yes, I can be clumsy, but I usually don't have to clean up a spill every day. Well, I can't say that anymore.

The amount of energy it takes to get through our days when we've been limited to external outlets is trying. There's bound to be some fallout. For me, one fallout is the inevitable dropping of at least one ball up in the air. Have any of us had to juggle so much while those around us are simultaneously juggling their own load? I doubt it. It's my first time on such a long haul.

The good enough news is that I am better prepared to clean it up. Though I'm more careful at the outset, it has not prevented me from spilling my coffee or dropping a jar of herbs. In the past, I've cursed and resented having to interrupt my flow to wipe up the mess. Now I see it as part of the process. Albeit a slow, dirty, frustrating process, but very much a part of this bumpy road we're on. We now can expect the unexpected. It might come in the form of a broken vase or a wet counter. Or, sadly, it might be in the form of a broken heart or an interrupted life. Sometimes a rag can do the trick. Other times a box of tissues is not enough to catch the tears we're shedding.

Let's have patience with ourselves and each other. There may not be a solution for what we're going through, but a kind word and a caring gesture can make all the difference in this messy era.

Self-Care Tips:

- When you drop something, take a breath. Give yourself a moment, then clean it up. Let the clean-up be its own activity.

- It's soup weather. Enjoy a new recipe. Rely on an old favorite. Or go out and purchase soup to warm up.

- Repeat this mantra for these times: "It's not what I wanted, but it's what I got."

- Go old school and create a collage. It can be a vision board, a creative venture, or make up your own theme.

- Find blue light glasses for your screen time.

WEEK THIRTY-FOUR:
Voter Anxiety

The stress of this election during the pandemic seems to have expanded as we move closer to Election Day. The conflicting commercials incite doubt and fear. The news is alarmist. And we're taking it all in. It felt empowering to vote, but it didn't last long.

We're living in a divisive environment. Many friendships have ended solely based on political preference. Families are divided over presidential partiality. Now that we're in the time of Coronavirus we get even more agitated when someone claims that they're voting for the opposition.

It's challenging to feel at peace now. With any luck, I feel it first thing in the morning and last thing at night between the time I get ready to meditate up until the moments of serenity following my meditation. Nature also elicits a feeling of calm. While here in the city, I walk through Central Park, Carl Shurz Park, and Randall's Island to enjoy the gifts of nature.

The rest of the day is a crap shoot. I may think I'm fine only to react to a seemingly insignificant interaction. It happened yesterday as I was walking Lucy, our dog. A woman got annoyed about our position on the sidewalk. And I responded in kind. I can't say why it was important for me to interact with her at all. But there I was, reacting unconstructively to a stranger. Conversely, there are many people I know who give me hope.

Friends, new and old, provide faith in the power of goodness. My family provides that too. They remind me of what's important. Common decency, a shared laugh at no one's expense, being heard, being understood, and a help-ing hand are all qualities I appreciate in my friends. Most of us will be preoccupied early this week. I know I'll be work-ing Tuesday, and when I'm done, I will most likely reach out to a couple of friends. It always feels good to affirm the power of kindness, especially now.

Self-Care Tips:

- Vote!

- Use a soft liquid soap or foam soap. It's a lovely, soothing experience in the shower and for your hands.

- Be curious. Listen up or view things from an inno-cent place to take in something new.

- Make a plan for election day. It's suggested you contact those who you find supportive.

- Check out the site, heathline.com, for voting safely.

WEEK THIRTY-FIVE:
Light Coming Through the Darkness

I hadn't realized how stressed I'd been these last four years until the presidential election results came in. My shoulders almost immediately released the tension I'd been holding. I felt lighter. Hopeful. The heavy months since the Coronavirus was revealed changed our world even further, adding to my stress. Mostly, I felt as if I was on the defensive, cautious when outside, and exhausted at home. In talking to so many other like-minded friends and family, I heard they, too, felt a collective sigh of relief Saturday.

I have no doubt that those who supported the president's reelection do not share our jubilation. They wanted something else. But I cannot endure more divisiveness. I don't want to live defensively anymore. I'm hopeful we can come together to create a change that is good for all of us.

It would be easy to wait for January to see what

happens. However, I believe in my heart that the first steps are not to count on leadership to make changes, but for each of us to start repairing the relationships that can bear the hard work in the name of peace. I know that I can do better at being gentle with myself when I get defensive. And, in turn, be kind to others, understanding they have their own pain.

We are not strong when we compare ourselves to others to feel better about ourselves. We are strong when we bring love, compassion, and consciousness to our relationships and our shared lives. I know I could stand to be less judgmental, and less reactive. I may not be able to stop altogether, but I can take steps, like pausing to ask myself what I'm feeling in that moment. Then attending to those feelings. We can start now to let the healing begin.

Self-Care Tips:

- Give yourself a moment of silence. See what it's like for you when you have that small space in time. What do you feel? Is it uncomfortable? What are your thoughts?

- Write down an apology. You don't have to send it. But write down something for which you are sorry. Then write what, if anything, will change now that you've apologized.

- Forgive. Think about someone or a situation for which you've held a grudge. See if you've already secretly forgiven that hurt. If so, acknowledge that for yourself.

- Take your vitamins either as part of the food you eat or as a supplement.

- **Be part of the solution.** Think of something that bothers you and take an action that brings you closer to an outcome you desire.

Time, Boredom & Patience

I woke up early this morning. My plan was to sleep in. But we all know what happens to plans in this time of the Coronavirus. I took advantage of the early hour to run to Central Park to slowly jog in the park. There are parts of my body that demand the slow pace. While runners and walkers passed me by, I chose patience for my leisurely stride. I admit there were moments I compared myself to other grey-haired runners who were twice as fast. Then I went back to kind self-talk as I slowly but surely went around the Park Drive and other paths.

The park looks beautiful. Though drawn out, my run was anything but boring. Yet, for many of us, boredom has set in during the pandemic. It's not the ennui of a lazy summer weekend; it's more of a dull lethargy. It's a feeling of "I don't wanna." It's a sensation many have day in and day out as we ride the Coronavirus wave.

Most of us thought that we would see a slight bump and then get back to our understanding of "normal." We all know that didn't happen. We're three-quarters of a year in, and we are still showing signs of impatience. The funny thing about time is that it can draw out our boredom. Time can also give us the space to incorporate patience.

As a child, I can't say that I really enjoyed the years I spent going to Shabbat services. I would squirm in my seat, waiting for the final benediction. Those hours spent in Synagogue, as well as the hours spent in school assemblies, and at the beauty parlor waiting for my mom to finish getting her bouffant, taught me how to sit still. They helped me to endure boring moments, and they allowed me the necessary time to learn patience.

I wasn't patient then. I'm still learning to be patient now. Without a lot of external distractions, I find that I'm more in tune with how I'm feeling, how I'm reacting, and how to care for myself in those moments. The pandemic has been so difficult in so many ways. Yet, one takeaway is that it has given me a chance to be a little more patient. And when I am patient with myself and my varying moods, then I have more patience for others. When things don't go my way, and there seems to be a lot of that in the pandemic, I rely on patience to get me through. It's a somewhat flawed system, because when I lack the patience to be patient with myself, then I have to find the patience for my impatient self.

Self-Care Tips:

- Go old school. Watch a movie from the 30s like Swing Time, 42nd Street, The Thin Man, or My Man Godfrey.

- Double down on old school by checking out stand-up comedians like Jack Benny, Richard Pryor, Lily Tomlin, Robin Williams, Moms Mabley, or Wendy Leibman.

- Find a noise, a hoot, an out loud, "yay," or something that's all your own to cheer you on for small wins during the day (i.e., Yay, I took a shower today).

- Take out the good China, silver, crystal. Sometimes we have to make any day a special day.

- Get a rescue remedy. It's the perfect Bach remedy for these times.

Thanksgiving, Gratitude & Disappointment

There's no doubt that this is a Thanksgiving like no other. Many will spend Thanksgiving, if it is being spent at all, without loved ones. In a large number of cases, it will be the first holiday without someone because they died, either of COVID-19 or from other causes. It's hard to feel thankful for these facts. We can embody gratitude for what we've had in the past. Or we may feel grateful for not having to be social when we're not up to seeing anyone. However, that's a far cry from the delight of festivities of past years.

Gratitude and its cousin, appreciation, can feel like a burden in times of fear, sadness, and loss. I am all for gratitude journals and gratitude as a tenet of living a deeply satisfying life. But we must come to this on our own terms. When Thanksgiving comes around, I find there's a collective social desire to manufacture gratitude on top of hardship. A kind of "fake it 'til you make it" premise. I propose that we are tender with the losses and disappointments of 2020. In telling the truth about what we have and what we don't have any more, or what we never had, we can find compassion for ourselves in these times. And if we can be grateful for anything, it is for our capacity to heal.

Self-Care Tips:

- Enjoy laughs. David Sedaris's new book, The Best of Me, is just what we need in these times. Hearing him read it in the Audible version adds to the pleasure.

- Consider the Buddhist tenet, "We are not our thoughts." When you are having thoughts that you don't like, or are uncomfortable, do a mental separation. Touch your hand and say, "This is me. That was a thought." You may have to repeat it a few times.

- Listen to jazz standards or other soothing music. I can recommend Natalie Douglas, Diana Krall, or Nancy Lamott.

- Hydrate. We tend to forget to drink water in the colder weather.

- Purposefully take a day off. If you can't do that, take short breaks, even if it means going to the bathroom alone and taking a couple of breaths before resuming your responsibilities.

The Desire for Instant Gratification

We made it through a very different Thanksgiving. Then, on Black Friday, I received so many emails advertising the "best" sales of the year. I was intrigued. I opened up a small business and non-profit website. I purchased a few things that I unquestionably don't need. Now, after the sale, I'm not even certain if they'll make good gifts. What I do know is that there was something compelling about the immediate gratification at a time when so little was happening. For a few brief hours, I'd take breaks to peruse websites while making a couple of impulsive purchases. Call it clearance therapy.

It felt like a small liberation to acquire a few seemingly needless items. The bargains were incredible. And it felt strange to engage in such a frivolous action. I understand that I'm privileged to buy stuff during this time of widespread unemployment. Perhaps I chose small businesses as an unconscious compensation. I like supporting solo endeavors, small businesses, and non-profit organizations. I grew up the daughter of a small business owner. Sale season was always a boon for his shoe store. The income from pre-holiday sales supported our family of six for the leaner times in the subsequent months. When I started working as a cashier at fourteen, I'd go to the mall and spend my earnings on the best sale offers I could find.

Perhaps it's part yearning for times past, and part needing something special we get to choose now. It's true that so many of us crave instant gratification during this long stretch. I got it Friday and will have another quick high when the packages arrive. During this pandemic, most of my immediate gratification came while walking. I'd see a beautiful light in the sky. Or the flowers would catch my eye. Actually, it was less immediate gratification than moments of grace. And, having had my clearance therapy on Friday, I was able to get back to walking and my slow running, enjoying the last colors of the season.

We're about to embark on living through the final month of 2020. We employed a tremendous amount of patience to get this far. And we're being asked to wait even longer before we'll be able to recognize certain aspects of pre-2020. I guess a few transgressions along the way are a small price to pay for getting through this time of the Coronavirus.

Self-Care Tips:

- Take in a poem. It helps us to imagine differently.

- Wear cozy socks. There's nothing like warm, comfortable socks as the weather gets cold. Try some with grips on the bottom to wear without shoes while indoors.

- Warm beverages can be so soothing. A favorite tea, hot cocoa, heated cider, or a warm adult beverage can all be enjoyed this season.

- Think of a personal quality that you judge unfavorably. Now think of a way in which that specific characteristic can be a strength under certain circumstances.

- Try adding a new color to your life. Whether you choose a different color for your mask, or you choose a vegetable that adds color to a meal, take pleasure in something different.

WEEK THIRTY-NINE:
Finding Joy

I found joy on a rainy day. Usually, when it rains in this pandemic, I've been apt to wane in energy. But when it was pouring outside this past week, I turned on an old dance playlist that Larry had previously made for me. It includes disco, Klezmer music, Irish folk music, jazz and so much more. I was in heaven. It's been so long since I've moved with utter abandon. There I was in my office, all alone, dancing for a good hour to song after song, gyrating and laughing. The power of music and movement is transformative.

I was slow to get out of bed as I felt the cool air while listening to the patter of the raindrops. Coffee helped, but it wasn't the power elixir I needed. At first, I tried to go out for a walk, but the rain and wind were strong, and I didn't want to start my workday wet. So, I found my Apple Music app. The last time I danced it was still called iTunes. The first song was Elvis singing "All Shook Up." That got me in the mood without hesitation. Luckily, I'm on the first floor, so no one was below me, allowing me to jump or spin when I was moved to do so.

In general, I've enjoyed small pleasures in this time of COVID-19. I pass unexpected winter flowers. Or I enjoy the cloud formations and light when the sky opens up between city buildings. Fun is relative in the pandemic. Yet, this past week's fun was full and joyous. Since I have hours of music, I'm going to dance again and again throughout the winter.

Self-Care Tips:

- Send holiday cards. We all need a little lift these days. And everyone enjoys receiving mail that's something other than bills or junk.

- Stamps. To send the cards go to USPS.com to find stamps that reflect you. Or create your own at Stamps.com.

- Call a friend. We're so used to using social media to get caught up. A person-to-person call is a lovely old-fashioned connection.

- Rub your feet. If you can reach them, try putting cream on the soles and rub it in. If bending down is difficult, rub your bare feet on a soft rug.

- Dance with abandon, alone, or with your pod.

WEEK FORTY:
Simple Pleasures

I was listening to early Joni Mitchell in the wee hours of the morning as the sun rose. Lucy and I were out for the first walk of the day. The weather is warm for December, and lovely in the tranquil dark. It was quiet, with the occasional runner or dog passing us as they started their day.

It's easy for me to recognize how special these moments are. As we make our way through this pandemic, I find that these ten months have worn on me. At this point, I really don't want to do anything. Which is all the more reason I am appreciative of every small pleasure I encounter. This morning it was being next to Lucy as she sniffed, and I watched the day begin. Now it's sitting down to write this as I enjoy a rare moment alone. Yesterday it was sitting with Alex. We didn't speak; we just enjoyed the company of one another. Earlier yesterday I was with Larry as sunset approached.

Although I am inclined to do less rather than more these days, I can go from thoroughly exhausted to deeply moved. My work day is filled with inspiring courage from those in my practice. Coming home from work I find an unexpected gift from a dear friend. Or I open up a holiday card, happy to think of the care that it took in sending it. There are so many moments of grace. As I reflect on these last months, I easily access the passionate emotions I've been navigating. My anger is fierce. My sadness pronounced. My foggy brain is a constant. And my appreciation of all the small pleasures, day in and day out, is pervasive. Thank you so much for taking the time to read this. You have given me the perfect gift in this time of the Coronavirus.

Self-Care Tips:

- Soup. It can be so soothing. I recommend Ina Garten's lentil soup recipe. Or, if you don't like to cook, try chicken broth with a touch of lemon juice.

- Try a new chapstick. I found one from Cococare that's lovely. It helps our lips in the winter, and it will feel soft under your mask.

- Thank someone today. It can be for something small like moving out of the way on the sidewalk. Or it can be a bigger thank you.

- Listen to the music that started you loving the singer, musician, piece, or group. It's so nice to revisit the awakening you had when you first heard it.

- If you spend time with others, find a quiet moment to savor. If you live alone, see if you can connect with someone who makes you smile.

WEEK FORTY-ONE:
Snow

Initially, there were grave warnings about the snowstorm that was going to plague the Northeast. When it started to fall, the winds were strong, and walking home from work was a bit of an effort. The following day there were hills with footsteps at the curbsides. Crossing the street took balance and navigation. Patience was needed, as only one person at a time could reach the next corner. Each person had their own pace, based on age, winter fitness, and foot-wear. Good snow boots were the best. So happy that past winters required me to find the right boots.

By Friday I was ready for a walk in the park. The park closest to me, Carl Shurz, had sledding children with their parents. It was hard to tell who was having more fun. The walkways were icy, so my time in the park was limited to dog walks. Central Park was more of a mix. The Park Drive was clear for walking and running. The side paths were too slippery to walk safely. So, I stuck to the Park Drive. From the Upper East Side, I could see snowmen and women being constructed. There was a couple cross-country skiing, displaying easy smiles. A snowball exchange spontaneously occurred. A great way to play while socially distanced.

Rather than the storm being a threat to the city, it provided a needed change to the atmosphere. Families had a reason to come out and play in the cold. Individuals were able to enjoy the scenery, as well as the dogs and people romping about. It lifted our moods. If anyone fell, strangers came to their rescue. Passing connections were found in these acts of kindness.

The sun's reflection on the snow adds brightness to our days. The light has melted some of the pain in these past months. The snow has been a gift in this time of Coronavirus.

Self-Care Tips:

- Look at the best of 2020 New Yorker cartoons on Instagram. Enjoy CBS's "Sunday Morning." Watch it in real time, record it, view it on demand. It always has positive messages; this week there's a segment on kindness.

- Shop in your closets. See if you can find something new, surprising, or an old favorite.

- Create a playlist for your chores.

- Go online to the USPS, United States Postal Service, and choose a Holiday wishlist to fulfill.

WEEK FORTY-TWO:
So Long 2020

Before the end of this week, we will welcome in a new year. Never will there have been a greater collective sigh throughout the globe than at the rotating midnight hour of 1/1/2021. We all faced many challenges throughout the year. And we all learned essential truths about ourselves. I learned that doing less was a relief. I learned that patience is not an endpoint but an ongoing process. I learned to use my crankier tendencies as a reflection on what vulnerabilities I am attempting to protect. I learned that I still have a lot to learn in asking for help. Plus, I learned that 2020 gave us endless opportunities to learn. I also learned that even with the possibility of learning, sometimes learning to relax was the best option.

Having to slow down gave me a chance to see the best in others. Family, friends, and others shared their kindness and generosity of spirit again and again. Courage rose exponentially as we faced multiple traumas. There was the courage to get through a single day. And there was the courage to recreate ourselves in the face of endless hardships.

I'm uncertain what the future brings. I long to travel, but don't want to go anywhere until we're all safe. I yearn for live theater; however, I can't say what that might look like post-pandemic. January 1st will look pretty much the same as the other days these past months. Nevertheless, I feel tremendous hope for our near future. We still have the beauty of nature, as long as we treat our natural world with respect. Thanks to acts of goodness and kindness, both apparent and unseen, we will continue to make it through this time of Coronavirus. Personally, I thank you for reading these blog posts. By giving your time and attention, you have been invaluable to me.

Self-Care Tips:

- Rather than looking for happiness, try working on feeling deeply satisfied.

- Instead of New Year's resolutions, think of what you'd like to let go of at the end of this year.

- Sleep, laugh, and cry. Not necessarily all together, but each provides relief and release.

- Review this past year and acknowledge all you accomplished, both large and small wins.

- Review this past year and celebrate the inner strengths you never knew you had.

WEEK FORTY-THREE:
Cautiously Optimistic

Is this really a Happy New Year? Yes, we survived 2020. And, yet, recalling how happy we were to be in a new decade just a year ago, we are constantly reminded of the unexpected turn of events in March.

In this first weekend of the new year, we take stock of the meaning of "hindsight is 2020." Relieved that 2020 is behind us, our memories are raw from all we witnessed, and all we faced personally. I now know the impact of ongoing stress on my body and mind. I am just beginning to understand what is required to soothe myself and support others going through the intensity of extreme tension. Sometimes it means reaching out and caring for someone, taking the attention off myself. Other times it means paying close attention to what I need, whether it be a nap, meditation, or another episode of Law & Order.

I am appreciative of the laughter brought to me by New Yorker cartoons, silly memes, posts on social media, and absurd memories with my sister, Sharyn. I have grown to love the color of the sky as I walk through the city streets and parks. I am grateful to my grandfather, Sam, who watched nature shows like The Mutual of Omaha's Wild Kingdom. Though I was bored as a child who preferred to see The Jetsons in those early years, now that I'm his age from that time, I appreciate the pleasure of seeing animals in their natural habitats on the small screen.

I have chosen not to make any resolutions. I am not resolving to be better in any way. Yes, I will work on bettering myself, but that remains a daily practice, one with many pitfalls and flawed attempts. And, this year, much like last year, I will pick myself up again and again, dust myself off, and slowly move ahead. If I remember, I will look up at the sky in child-like wonderment. A moment of awe, whatever year it might be.

Go gently into 2021, step by small step.

Self-Care Tips:

- Alternate self-care behavior. This way you find what works best, and what you need in different situations.

- If and when you feel aches or pains, touch the area with care. This is not a substitute for medical care; please attend to that. This is a small gesture that affirms the healing power of touch.

- Rather than thinking of all you will do in 2021, think of what you will no longer do. Find the joy of saying "no thank you" to one or two "shoulds."

- Lower your expectations. We've lived with a lot of disappointments this past year. Lowering our expectations allows us to take in and act on what comes our way.

- Try something new, or try anything you're not good at, like a new recipe, trying your hand at poetry, or learning a new language. It helps us to develop humility.

WEEK FORTY-FOUR:
Boy, Oh, Boy

Yesterday, I hit the wall. Before I lost all steam, I had lofty plans. I had research to do. There is always cleaning and organizing. I was behind on my writing. Yet, by the time I was three-fourths of the way through a walk in Central Park, I felt as if I was dragging my leaden legs on the southern arc of the Reservoir. When I finally reached home, I couldn't get my sweats on fast enough. Then Lucy had to go out. I love her, and also dearly wished there was someone else who would have taken her out. I was able to speak with a friend from the other coast, and that gave me a pleasurable energy shot. However, life in California is as fraught as it is in New York and throughout the world.

This past week brought to the forefront the negative results of anger and hate. Those are human experiences, but when those feelings are unchecked, then further fueled, they become destructive. I hope we can learn from this rather than take sides with defensive righteousness. I certainly see how my own unexamined anger hurts Larry, Alex, and probably others. Once I see that I've hurt them, I have to consider what changes I can make so that we share joy rather than pain. It's an ongoing process of patience and kindness mixed with tools to calm my agitated soul.

Was it possible I had no energy to calm myself after Wednesday's attack on the Capitol? That played a part in my exhaustion; nonetheless, having witnessed it from afar, it's not the only reason. From what I've heard, I am not alone in running out of steam in this time of Coronavirus. We are all frayed. We have been faced with challenges that have pushed us beyond our known limits, while still having to conduct our lives on a daily basis.

I imagine yesterday's pause was essential. It meant I missed attending my first Zoom party. It was only this morning that I even remembered that it was last night. I think of my friends and family daily. I so appreciate what they are doing to brighten others' lives. Though it's an internal reflection since I rarely reach out these days, I am grateful that they are in the world and my thoughts.

Here we go into another week. What will it bring? We'll see. For me, I plan to get more rest. I'm hopeful that will make room for added patience and kindness.

Self-Care Tips:

- Light a candle. Whether it's a small birthday candle or a luxurious scented candle, light a candle to brighten these dark winter nights.

- Compliment someone. It's easy to think nice thoughts, but it's invaluable for someone to hear that you noticed.

- Look up. Sometimes we see things we would have otherwise missed.

- Go for a walk, short or long; it can be an essential calming tool.

- Pause. Check your breath and survey your body. Coming back to ourselves, even thirty seconds at a time, is another way of acquiring calm.

WEEK FORTY-FIVE:
What We Don't Know

I have to admit that I wasn't sure that the judge I watched numerous times on Law & Order was Fran Lebowitz. It looked like her, but was she a doppelganger, or was she, in fact, the writer? After watching "Pretend it's a City," Martin Scorsese's excellent (in my opinion) docu-series of Fran Lebowitz, I was happy to learn that, yes, it was her as Judge Janice Goldberg in the original Law & Order.

The short series on Netflix was a delightful, laughter-filled escape from current events this past week. I learned a lot, evaluated my own thinking, and admired FL's ability to speak her personal truths, thoughts I often have but don't share aloud. Somehow, the cable show also had me pondering on the wonder of all I don't know. I'm not even sure how I arrived at that thought trend, but once there, my mind wandered endlessly to all that is yet to be explored. I'm not speaking of subjects that vaguely interest me, but not enough to occupy my time, like physics or economics. I'll leave that to the experts. Then I'll simply read their selective theories. I'm more thinking about what curiosities I can discover in a day, in a new place, or with those who think differently than myself. Am I willing to let go enough to be in awe of the newness of an experience, much like a young child? I'm willing to try. I'll see how it goes. If nothing else, I'll learn more about my curiosity or lack thereof.

I can't say I was in child-like wonderment while I tried to learn two new computer programs today. It was more like initial confusion followed by adult frustration. My curiosity quickly morphed into baffled exasperation. Though I wasn't as open as I would have liked, I was able to marvel at my reaction, and my limited ability to take in perplexing information. I will try again briefly today, but it appears I need more time and energy to learn these programs. May I say that the tutorials for both wrongly claim the ease in which one can get them up and running. What I didn't fully appreciate before is that I cannot rely on old knowledge to magically create an aptitude for new skills.

It helped to admit that I couldn't figure out how to launch the programs. Though I was hoping not being able to master the first program, I could figure out the second one. Not having the bandwidth to take in anything new happens more now in the pandemic. And, if that's not enough, even old facts leave me with limited mental access. If I once knew something but can't recall it at a particular time, I'm more embarrassed than if I never knew it at all. Or, if I am familiar with a topic but know no specifics about said topic, I've been reluctant to admit that. I am happy to eschew that behavior by proudly admitting all I don't know. I certainly don't know how this will go, but I'm curious to find out. In the meantime, I'll reread Fran Lebowitz's essays.

Self-Care Tips:

- Admit that you don't know something. It's better to learn by not knowing than to be uncertain of what you might know.

- Make room for making mistakes; it's bound to happen, and it helps us grow.

- Shape recommendations or suggestions to accommodate your life rather than shaping your world to acclimate to specific advice.

- Watch Netflix's "Pretend it's a City," or something else true to your sense of humor.

- Place a light fragrance on your wrist, and sniff it periodically to get you through tough times.

WEEK FORTY-SIX:
You Never Know

Sometimes I find myself quick to judge. I hear a whiny individual at a Zoom meeting, and I silently groan. I also know that there have been times, and I chance to say there are still times, in which I am the one who warrants another's groan. In my more open-minded moments, I remember that everyone is trying the

best they can. We are all going through this pandemic, and there's nothing easy about that. But there are other times when my exhaustion and impatience take over, and I am unforgiving of anyone who annoys me; from the selfishly maskless to virtual-meeting squeaky wheels.

Something I've noticed recently in my professional and personal life is how instantaneously we jump from one emotional state to another. As quick as I am to criticize and sigh, I am equally swift to be moved by others' suffering now. When I open up to the sheer humanity of getting through each day in this time of Coronavirus, it is awe-inspiring.

Not only are we plodding as best we can day in and day out, but so many have faced hardships that would bring tears to our eyes if we only knew. But we do not know. It's easy for me to judge someone based on my own needs and preferences. In those moments I forget that they are struggling in their own way, as I grapple with life in my way.

I have heard people imagine how much easier it is for others. I have listened to their envy. What I do know is that while others may enjoy specific circumstances, they are not immune to suffering. No one is completely protected from the world's ills. Let's try to tease out our opinions from our innate compassion. They do not have to be mutually exclusive. I will probably continue to remain judgmental in certain ways. Nonetheless, I hope to remember not to take myself too seriously. I hope to remember others live with a story that would take my breath away. We all live with our stories.

Self-Care Tips:

- Write positive affirmations on post-it notes and place them on shelves, in drawers, and in cabinets. This way you get positive messages throughout your home. Examples of positive affirmations are, "You matter," "Focus on your gifts," or "You're awesome."

- Create an avatar for your anxiety. When you have racing thoughts or anxious thinking, draw or digitally create an avatar. Like in a comic book, have the avatar say the things you're thinking.

In this way, it places the anxious thoughts outside of you, making them potentially easier to address.

- If you listen to the news, try reading it for a day. See if it feels different to read about current events rather than being told.

- Set an alarm on your calendar to laugh. Find something funny on YouTube, read a joke, or enjoy a cartoon. We all need a daily laughter break.

- When you judge another, also leave space in your mind to appreciate that the person has his/her/their own struggles.

WEEK FORTY-SEVEN:
Pandemic Envy

We have become accustomed to the average pandemic envy, like seeing those who prepare feasts as a way to get through this time of Coronavirus. Many of us have felt jealousy of acquaintances in larger homes. The more exhausted have longed for the energy cited in posts of new hobbies or accomplishments. Some parents envy those with no children or those with safe help for their families. A number of people who feel alone have been envious of those who post happy couple or family portraits. Individuals who feel trapped with their families begrudge others who they imagine live blissfully alone. Now add to that the newer vaccine envy.

Without distractions, I'm able to feel my emotions strongly. Sometimes this can be therapeutic. I can soothe myself if I'm agitated, or enjoy the moment when calm is present. However, there are other times when I look for diversions. It's not easy to feel everything all the time, and even more so in this time of the Coronavirus. When I do look away at distracting social media posts, I find myself envious of how some others are getting through the pandemic.

How do they find time to work out so much? Their meals look amazing. Why aren't they sharing how hard this is? How is it that they are thriving in ways I can only imagine? These are some of the thoughts I've had. I understand that what I see and read on social media and in print is merely one sliver of what another is experiencing. I wish I could appreciate all that I have and simply be happy for them. Alas, I am still working on that.

More recently, there have been many instances when individuals have shared that they got their vaccines, only to be met with others who are desperate to receive theirs. The rollout has been anything but equitable. Many are working at essential jobs and are not able to log in repeatedly to obtain a prized time slot. Others found their dates were canceled. The ongoing uncertainty fuels vaccine envy. If you feel vaccine envy, you're not alone. Hopefully, all of us who want the vaccine can get it soon so we can move on from fear to well-being.

Self-Care Tips:

- Snuggle. If you have a pet and they are amenable, snuggle with them. If not, snuggle with a willing partner, or find a stuffed animal to snuggle. You're never too old. Or, if you prefer, a cozy blanket, comforter, or pillow can stand in as a snuggle item.

- When feeling envious, slow down and name some things for which you are grateful.

- If you feel vaccine envy, if you have the time, investigate what sites are opening up spots, then share it with others. In NYC there are vaccine sites, as there are in other parts of the country.

- Dress in layers for the cold weather. If you're able, wear glove liners and thermal or silk underwear.

- Use hand and body cream. It's great for the cold weather, and rubbing yourself with the cream is a soothing act.

WEEK FORTY-EIGHT:
Ennui

Again and again, I hear from others, "I'm so over this." Of course, this refers to the pandemic and its related restrictions. Yes, we need to lessen the spread of COVID-19, yet that doesn't mean we're happy about what's required. Now, even with the spotty vaccine rollout, we are expected to buckle down more so with the presence of new strains, which, in turn, places new stressors on us. With added stressors, any energy we have burns quicker. We are exhausted and might feel resentment, anger, or woe. This is what has happened in the daily grind without proper reprieves.

I am certainly dragging my feet. Whether it's writing this blog or cooking a meal, I lack whatever eagerness I had in past years. I have no get-up-and-go these days. And I know I'm not alone. I whine silently in my head, "I don't wanna." Fill in the blank __________ because "I don't wanna" can signify pretty much anything. This doesn't mean I don't experience joy. There are small moments that turn "I don't wanna" upside-down.

I am pleased and surprised when I delight in an unexpected moment. It could be anything from watching a healthcare worker, still in scrubs, coming home from a long day caring for others, to the subtle evening sky light in between high rises. Those are moments that give me pause, then move me forward. Conversely, seeing the messy surfaces at home on shelves, table tops, or cabinets stops me in my tracks as I sigh with resignation.

Moving forward is a slow process in this time of Coronavirus. It's not always easy to discern when we must succumb to the "I don't wannas," and when we can kindly take a step toward the next matter of business. I probably won't be able to organize my home while working and carving out self-care through the pandemic. And I may not be able to fool around in the kitchen to cook as often, either. Nevertheless, I will enjoy those pleasurable moments when they show up, your kind likes and comments included.

Self-Care Tips:

- Ask yourself, "How am I doing?" It's always good to check in.

- Then ask, "What do I need that's attainable now?" It's helpful to know what you need and what you can have.

- Enjoy the gentle sensation of a soft toothbrush.

- Find or get a smooth stone to rub during stressful moments, or while on Zoom calls. If you can get one in your favorite color, do that.

- Take quick dance breaks. Turn on a song and move. It breaks up the ennui.

WEEK FORTY-NINE:
Love in the Time of Coronavirus

I wish you a Happy Valentine's Day. In doing so, I am very aware that Valentine's Day is loaded. Maybe even more so in the pandemic. Here in New York restaurants are now open for indoor dining. Some will make it a romantic evening. Some will fight because they have very different safety parameters. Some will feel lonely as they have in years past. Some will be uniquely solo in this COVID-19 year. Many will measure others' love by what attention they receive or don't receive today. And others will see it as just another Sunday. Whatever the case, Valentine's Day is signified by hearts, the social sign of love.

Love is a peculiar thing. We read about it, we say, "I love you," and we're told to love ourselves. And, yet, love is not a measurable commodity. We have seen love take so many forms in the pandemic. My expression of love has been everything from open and joyous to thorny and messy. My acceptance of others' love has been a balm at times. While other times I have been judgmental and closed-minded.

We often learn that love looks a particular way. And when those who love us express it in another form, it can feel invalidating. They may not love us any less, but it's hard to take it in when it looks different than our expectations. And, loving ourselves is a whole other ballgame. Often it feels like loving ourselves is a consolation for not receiving the love we want.

Nevertheless, I believe that loving ourselves is exactly the love we need. When we are gentle while vulnerable, kind when stressed, and caring when upset, then we are both providing ourselves with the love we need and taking in the love we're giving. How wonderful is that? It may feel painful that we experience that alone. If so, then the kindness we impart will go a long way.

I am going to do the best I can to be kind to myself. I am committed to being kind to those I love, those I like, and to strangers. My kindness will be imperfect. I tend to be moody, and I don't always have the emotional fortitude to express a generosity of heart. But I will do my best. And, as I accept the love given to me, and accept my limitations, as well as those of others, I will see that acceptance as an act of love. This is not necessarily what I was taught about love; it is what I've learned since then.

Self-Care Tips:

- Give yourself a break from self-care. Sometimes it can become an obligation rather than a caring act. When that's the case, take a pause.

- Chapstick or lip balm, in your favorite flavor if you like, can be restorative on dry winter days.

- Shelf-care. Go through your books. See if there are any you've meant to read and take them off the shelf. Or see what you can give away.

- Watch a James Corden video on YouTube. May I suggest a Carpool Karaoke? He aims to bring laughter.

- Celebrate a party of One. You are number one. And celebrating yourself in any manner that brings delight is the perfect party.

Let's Be Real

As we approach a year in semi-lockdown we've been filled with powerful emotions. Social niceties often elude us as we exchange suspicious looks with masked strangers. We don't have to dig deep to touch upon anxiety or aggravation; they are neatly placed on the surface of our emotional reservoirs. Our tolerance level has been masterfully challenged. And at times our sustained tolerance is losing ground. Well-wishers tout positivity. I am all for optimism. Heck, I write my blog with self-care tips. But when we're on the edge, as we often find ourselves in this pandemic, the last thing we want to hear is how lucky we are.

When I feel blue, I'm resistant to hearing that I should be grateful for what I have. And, if we're being real, most of us have had blue periods in this time of Coronavirus. I'm not saying that gratitude isn't important. I have an active daily practice of gratitude, and it's been invaluable. But I do believe that we have to be where we are. When we force gratitude or self-care on ourselves or others, we negate the real experience in that moment. I know things are tough when I'm easily annoyed by little slights. Telling me to let it go just adds to my exasperation. If we're going to find hope or gratitude at all, we have to start with where we are. We can't always make the leap to positivity because someone else is uncomfortable with our irascibility.

When we are able to acknowledge the hardships and upset that we're experiencing, then we can move on from there. Each of us deals with this differently. Sometimes I can yell into a pillow, cry, and take a walk. And in doing those things, I find myself in a lighter place. Other times it takes a good night's sleep. Or I need to talk in therapy or to a friend. When I do, I have the wherewithal to be delighted by small kindnesses. Just this week strangers made room for narrow paths in the snow, and neighbors waited at the open door while I carried in my groceries. It was lovely. Their kindness allowed for an ease of gratitude. When I have the bandwidth, I, too, will do what I can to ease someone else's load. And, when I don't, I'll do my best to have patience with myself, remembering that we're living through a pandemic.

Self-Care Tips:

- Create a list of complaints. Sometimes we need to unload. Be a complainer; write down what bothers you. Give voice to your agitation. If it helps, tear it up or cut it up, then throw it out with force.

- Growl, sigh, and exhale loudly. Sounds give voice to our unheard feelings. (If you live with others, warn them first.)

- I delight in _______ (fill in the blank).

- See if there is a way to make room for whatever you filled in above. If not, see if there are any first steps you can take to have or do whatever you delight in.

- Stop what you're doing. Pause. Ask yourself, "How am I doing?" It's always good to check in with yourself. It's good information to have even when you can't take action to address it.

WEEK FIFTY-ONE:
Insult to Injury, 2020 Taxes

I like scrambled eggs. They are soft and comforting. However, when my mind is scrambled, I find no comfort in that. These past two weekends, I've endeavored to do my taxes. Doing taxes in the time of Coronavirus is less than optimal. That said, I am going to take a nap. An afternoon siesta is not a usual practice, especially when slogging through last year's numbers. In the past, I've faced the forms down and I got through it, complaining while I add up sums and input data. Today is different. I don't have the wherewithal. I'm having difficulty focusing. Taxes in a pandemic is another ridiculously compulsory task we're forced to endure.

Nap completed, and I've taken a brief refuge in writing this now. I see the calculator staring me down, so I'll have to resume my taxes in a little while. When I do, I imagine

I'll go slowly. I'd love to rush through it. But having made mistakes in the past, I prefer slow and steady to the headache of a future audit.

Because it's a rainy day, I am less inclined to venture out, making this a theoretically perfect day for paperwork. But as far as I'm concerned, paperwork is a necessary evil, not a respectful task worth my time and energy. Taxes aren't fun. At least that's been my experience.

I didn't always feel that way. There was a time a few decades ago when I was proud of my record-keeping and my ability to have organized files. It wasn't until I worked for others as a side hustle, helping with their bookkeeping, that I found out that I had deluded myself with my organizational skills. My acumen with an adding machine was deeply flawed. I missed receipts and tabulated sums incorrectly. My false confidence was exposed.

I have no such confidence now. Nor do I wish to acquire it. I respect others who excel in bookkeeping and accounting. This is their season to shine. Kudos to them. I hope to complete my taxes in the next two weeks, when I will send them off to our wonderful accountants. For now, though, I will go back to the numbers. And I think I'll have scrambled eggs for dinner to comfort me when I'm done for the day.

Self-Care Tips:

- Change up your routine. Try to do things differently for a fresh perspective.

- When going into an unwanted situation, place a few dabs of a scent you like on your wrists or other points so you can take in the aroma when things get tough.

- When multitasking, see if there's a way to focus on one task and get some or all of it done before moving on to the next task. This gives you a better chance of having a sense of satisfaction with your work.

- Shred. It can feel great to get rid of old papers.

- Do the hokey pokey and turn yourself around. That's what it's all about.

WEEK FIFTY-TWO:
Oh, The Memories

This is the last week of a full year of social distancing, and all that comes with it. Most of us are ready to finish this disruptive chapter and return to the activities we love. Yet, I imagine there will come a time in the future when we will wax nostalgic for this time.

Perhaps we'll appreciate the safety of wearing masks, not just to protect ourselves from COVID-19 but because we had fewer colds or cases of influenza. We will yearn for a ready-made excuse for plans we prefer not to attend. We will crave long walks in the middle of the day. We will appreciate the rare times when family members in the house laughed together at silly moments. We will hunger for communion with nature on a regular basis. We will long for a simpler time, like we've been experiencing now.

We all discovered, had we not known before, the public

value of toilet paper, the comfort of everyday yoga pants, and the ease of simply staying in. We found comfort in our surroundings. The delight of first blooms. The joy of open spaces, a river view. And we found solace in the small wins. In losing so much in the span of this pandemic year, we gained a deep appreciation that less is more. We'll see how this plays out in the coming months. And it will be interesting to see when we become sentimental about the lessons learned in the time of Coronavirus.

Self-Care Tips:

- Ask yourself, "Is there anything I need?" Answer as honestly as you can. You may discover there are needs not addressed. Or you may find that you are taking care of yourself better than expected. Whatever the answer, checking in with yourself is a reminder of your importance.

- Think of a situation in which being right became the be-all and end-all. If possible, see if you can shift to compassion and apologize for not appreciating the other's perspective.

- Note an insecurity of yours. Now see if there is an upside for something that feels bad to you (i.e., I used to cry a lot and thought I was too sensitive; now I use my sensitivity to appreciate music, joy, and empathy).

- Choose an item at home that elicits a specific memory. See if you can remember the experience, then assess if you might feel freer should you be able to discard or give away that item.

- Enjoy a soundtrack from a beloved film of the past. It will envelop you in euphony and nostalgia.

WEEK FIFTY-THREE:
What a Year

I am befuddled. The last thing I need is an hour of lost sleep. And, yet, one less hour of living in a pandemic sounds pretty good. The common rationale for the perpetuation of daylight savings time is extended daylight. Sunlight has been invaluable to us these past twelve months. Sunrises, sunsets, and the shades of illumination while outdoors have provided medicinal assets in this time of Coronavirus. So, we will sacrifice an hour's sleep for lighter days.

Daylight savings time comes as we note an anniversary we could never have imagined. We didn't want to mark the passing of this previous pandemic year. I've been hearing about the discomfort that can't be explained as our bodies feel the weight of this past year deep in our cells. Many of us have felt "off." I forgot to answer important emails. I was a bit achy, walking slower than usual. But the walks helped, as they always do.

Aside from the events and socialization we missed this past year, we are equally missing acquaintances and arbitrary human contact. Even on my walks, while I pass people, mask-wearing has obscured some fundamental assessment of others. Not only do I not recognize most people, even the regular park dwellers, but for me, the masks obscure my mind's ability to gauge the whole picture. Although I cherish some parts of this newfound anonymity, I don't like the absence of fully assessing the moods and characters of those around me.

The simple day-to-day acknowledgment from one human to another has been significantly curtailed. There have been limited or no interactions that are merely casual. We miss those who we saw at the stores we frequented. We miss the service people who we might have seen infrequently, but who we came to expect when the circumstance arose. We miss speaking to strangers. Well, perhaps we miss the option to speak with certain strangers. And most of us miss the everyday familiarity we came to expect on our commutes, our routines, and our outings.

Perhaps now that the days are longer and the sun brighter, I will attempt to look above the masks into strangers' eyes, enjoying the sun sparkling off them. Pre-pandemic, looking into the eyes of strangers was deemed rude. Now, it is how we smile at one another. I may not take in the big picture, so I will rely on a small snapshot of the light, the eyes, and a passing connection with Spring in the air.

Self-Care Tips:

- Play. We forget to play, thinking that's a child's business. Yet, celebrating our child within can be pure joy.

- Quit. If there is something you think you should be doing but you really don't want to, and it's a specific requirement you put on yourself, just leave it. I've been quitting books I don't like.

- Move. Sitting at our desks or having a static position can cause stiffening. Move a bit; whether you go for a run, simply sway your arms, or do the twist, it all helps to loosen us up.

- Hug. If you live alone, stretch your arms around your torso and give yourself a hug. If you live with others, and both you and they are amenable, exchange a nice hug.

- Talk. Go to therapy. Talk to a friend. Contact a family member. Tell your truth.

WEEK FIFTY-FOUR:
Love & Hardship

Throughout this past week, I heard how difficult the week was. We had all gone through a year milestone, but there would be no celebrating. How do we celebrate one year of a pandemic? We don't. We hunker down, as we had for over fifty-two weeks, and trudge on. It has been recommended that when we feel particularly vulnerable, that is the best time to incorporate a self-care and self-love practice. And, though I share self-care tips, all of which I either try or do on a regular basis, self-love and self-care can feel like ephemeral notions.

Self-love and self-care are phrases bandied about as if being able to understand the phrases gives us magical powers in living a life full of love and care toward ourselves. I, however, think these ideas often stay conceptual because we are told to just do this or that and it will all be okay. It is my belief that we have to rethink self-love and self-care.

I used to imagine love meant 100% acceptance of the loved. More often than not, I pushed down feelings of sadness, anger, frustration, and bewilderment. My thinking was, "How can I truly love them if I feel this or that? I better learn to be more accepting." So, I moved forward with shame and self-rage so that I could be a "loving" person. I attended to their requirements, or at least I thought I did, while I eschewed my own needs. Not only was this the opposite of self-love, but it was a misattunement of all love.

When we deny ourselves the space to feel all our feelings, then we block kindness and care towards ourselves and others. Love, more often than not, is imperfect. We've all seen this as we distance in place. Cohabitating for long stretches without diversions means we witness the best and worst in each other day in and day out. If we live alone, then we are grateful for any contact, sometimes even when it leaves us wanting.

When I say how important it is to give ourselves the space to feel our feelings, I do not mean that we are free to rage or dump those feelings on others. Sometimes I share my love by not sharing my thoughts. I silently acknowledge this act of generosity. In this way, I have the room to experience my feelings, but I am not compelled to hurt someone else, even at those times I want them to hurt like I hurt.

The great thing about love and care is that it is an evolving practice. When we are hard on ourselves, perhaps for not being as caring as we think we should be, like when we want someone to hurt like we're hurting, then we can double down on patience and kindness for attempting the difficult. Perfection and the determination to reach perfection get in the way of living and loving fully. Now that we have passed the one-year mark of living in the COVID-19 pandemic, let's applaud our grit. Let's celebrate our imperfect love. Let's appreciate whatever self-care we've been able to incorporate. Let's acknowledge how hard this has been. Let's commend all we've learned about love, care, kindness, and patience. Yay, us!

Self-Care Tips:

- Daydream. Let your mind go. These breaks are essential, not only for creativity but for survival at difficult times.

- Savor breakfast. Sometimes we want our day to start so we have whatever we can in the morning. Truly enjoying our first meal is a lovely foundation for the day.

- Chew slowly. We can really relish our food by slowing down and chewing slowly. It lowers our stress and supports us in being in the moment.

- Find a new source of humor. Laughter remains invaluable. Ask those who share a similar sense of humor if they can recommend a show, a comedian, a video, or anything else that will make you laugh.

- Take a picture. Whether you want to document a moment, beauty, or something meaningful, a photograph allows you to revisit it again and again.

WEEK FIFTY-FIVE:
How Are You?

It's a rainy Sunday, overcast and wet outside. I ventured out early to capture the sunrise on the East River; instead, I was welcomed with grey clouds and mist. Beautiful in its subtlety, but not as majestic as even a partially cloudy day. A day like today can be difficult for those going through hardships, the bereaved, the infirmed, caregivers, those suffering from mental illness, parents with young children, parents with older children, the lonely, and anyone else who is dealing with their own life struggles. One of the worst questions, yet most often asked, is, "How are you?" How do we answer that in a pandemic?

When we ask, "How are you?" we see a slight hesitation before the respondent says, "Fine." The habitual question and answer are from pre-pandemic times. It's automatic, but not currently. I make mistakes from time to time and ask how someone is doing. I then double back and qualify it by inquiring, "How are you given the pandemic?" At least then I'm acknowledging some hardship in our present reality. Nonetheless, the question remains flawed. Perhaps we can find other ways to connect.

We can ask, "What's new?" I'm joking. What's really new when we're still socially distanced? I'm more inclined to ask, "What are you reading?" "What are you watching?" "What are you enjoying these days?" "Do you cook or order in?" "Anything you can recommend?" I ask all of these to assess how my friends, colleagues, and family are doing.

I remember a neighbor who used to ask how I was. I'd always say, "Fine." However, her ask was more of an invitation to ask her how she was. When she answered, she was long-winded. It surpassed the parameters of polite neighbor banter and leaped into intrusive and annoying. Needless to say, I smile politely when I see her now, but I pass by quickly with no curiosity about her state of being. I merely feel relief that I dodged her socially-inappropriate bullet. Maybe we all feel a sigh of relief for the absence of similar encounters.

How are we? We're tired, we're grateful, we're sad, we're joyful, we're frustrated, we're patient, we're absent-minded, we're mindful, we're angry and we're peaceful. It's a veritable bouillabaisse of emotions. Perhaps no different than pre-2020, but probably more noticeable than in our recent past. Even so, we may not be able to tease out one feeling from another at any given moment. So please refrain from asking, "How are you?"

Self-Care Tips:

- When speaking to someone, rather than asking them how they are, try another question or phrase. You could say, "Good to speak with you, or see you." Or "Tell me what bores you these days?"

- Write lists and cross-off items as needed. We've been forgetting things, so writing lists helps us to see what to do and what we can forget about doing.

- Watch "In and Of Itself." It's a magical theatrical performance now available on Hulu.

- Be silly.

- Find an app like www.myfridgefood.com to make quick, easy recipes for ingredients already in your pantry and refrigerator.

WEEK FIFTY-SIX:
Hello Again, Spring

This past week proved to be particularly challenging for so many of my clients, as well as friends and colleagues. Walking through the city brings a needed brightness as the early signs of Spring appear. The warm air feels fresh. The cooler air keeps the parks emptier. Either has its benefits.

Though we've become accustomed to our pandemic routines, it seems unbelievable that we're beyond a year in the time of Coronavirus. As with all things far-fetched, it takes time and repetition to integrate the reality of these circumstances. We got through the past year (plus a few weeks) by imagining a time beyond the pandemic. At present, though, we're left with an uncertainty that belies our peace of mind.

I am counting on the same anchors to continue getting through this. The sun rises every day. When I'm awake in time, I go to the East River to start my day. The beauty envelops me, and I let it. Though I don't get a good view of sunsets, I do appreciate the changing light at dusk that I witness when facing west. And I always appreciate the photographs of others' sunsets when posted.

Then there's meditation. Some days it's as if I'm being lifted up. Other mornings meditating feels like a long time to be with a racing mind. Similar to a gratitude journal. Some days my heart is open, and then there are the days when I have to push for appreciation of simple things. I have so much for which to be grateful, but exhaustion and a hazy mood sometimes get the better of me.

We've learned a lot during this time. Though I adore the city, it has been nature that grounds me, providing peace and joyful moments. I have learned the importance of rest. Prior to March 2020, I took advantage of all the city had to offer. I lived by the Warren Zevon credo, "I'll Sleep When I'm Dead." Now I'm sleeping, napping, being still, resting, or simply taking it easy to enjoy living as best I can.

This year has slowed me down. There is still so much to get done, but my to-do list is less important than listening to friends and family, doing the work I love, and looking up at the sky. Glad that Spring is in the air.

Self-Care Tips:

- Take a break. Sometimes stepping away is the best choice.

- Find a small smooth stone to rub when you need soothing.

- Try flavored salts. They add another dimension to dishes.

- When noticing a behavior or habit you don't like, rather than judge, ask what might be happening that prompted the behavior and bring compassion.

- Look up at the sky and enjoy the sun, the clouds, the stars, and the moon.

WEEK FIFTY-SEVEN:
Foggy

It's foggy this morning. How apropos for these times. Our minds are foggy. Well, mine is. By the end of any given day, I have limited access to names and words. If I want to relax in the evening, I'm challenged to remember one of a number of shows I enjoy watching.

It also seems foggy when we think of moving forward. We are slowly making our way back to a life previously known. I'd love to travel, dine out, and enjoy theater. Yet, I am more cautious now, valuing health and safety over social luxuries. Presently, travel consists of walking to Central Park. Though today I moved through the fog to Randall's Island, where I soon got lost. It was a bit of a challenge not being able to find my bearings since distance visibility was obliterated by low clouds.

In general, this morning's walk is very much how I'm getting through these days in the time of Coronavirus. I can't see anything in the distance, so I'm reliant on what is right in front of me. What's right in front of me is quite simple. I work. I write. I prepare simple meals. I eat. Larry and I laugh when I'm not being defensive or critical. I walk. If I'm feeling really adventurous, I take out my bike. Every morning I meditate. Every night I sleep, lucky if I do it well enough. Of course, there are other things that fill my days, but my brain is foggy, and I can't think of much more now.

As the haze of the pandemic continues to blanket our days, we will take one step at a time to find our way to safer ground. Are we there yet? No. But we're steps closer. Given all we've been through, we can trust our ability to persist through the mist.

Self-Care Tips:

- Nostalgia! Throwback to another time.

- Listen to music you enjoyed at a younger age.

- Play a game that used to be fun for you.

- Find scents that elicit positive memories, whether it's from a bakery, a freshly mowed lawn, or from a family member's fragrance tray.

- Delight in a childhood comfort food.

WEEK FIFTY-EIGHT:
Individualism

I've been confused. I thought I knew myself. Instead, who I knew was a woman who was highly influenced by the world around me. This wasn't necessarily a bad thing; it just wasn't representative of the totality of me. We've all been there. Whether we're enticed by a product commercial, or whether we want to join in on experiences with those who surround us, we make choices based on an outside influence. Sometimes this works to our advantage. I've visited beautiful places based on recommendations. I've also spent a good amount of money on things I didn't need and ultimately didn't want.

There are some things that have been a constant. I knew what I liked: theater, work, blueberry crumb muffins. I knew what I didn't like: loud noises like relentless car horns in stuck traffic, or people who take up the entire sidewalk, making it impossible to pass. Nothing has changed on those fronts. Yet, I have noticed that I am much more tolerant now of the unlikable items on my shortlist.

I like my garden much more than in the past. I'm enjoying it more, too. I'm a squeamish gardener at best. For some reason, getting my hands dirty is not fun for me. For instance, as much as I love lobster, I am no fan of pulling it apart to secure the tender meat. But choosing flowers and enjoying a small and rare patch of green in the city is as good as it gets while I find my way back into the larger world.

I'm also much more appreciative of the small things. Kindness, whether from a friend who reaches out or a stranger who keeps a door open, means so much to me. I am grateful for Alex's late-night texts filled with bad jokes and lots of love. I am grateful that Larry washed the dishes last night after a long day at work. He did it without me asking, or even before I could complain that I had one more thing to do.

There are many things that I would not have known about myself had the world not changed drastically. Surprisingly, birds have been nice to see. In the past, I appreciated the bright red cardinals I'd pass, but I was nonplussed by other avian varieties. Now, when walking in the park, I look up to see all sizes and colors of birds, enjoying the brief sitting as I move through the now leafy spaces. Most importantly to me, I'm not missing the many activities that defined my evenings. I assumed I'd be bored if I did less. Not so. I am better rested. I feel more grateful. Letting go feels easier.

An unexpected benefit of this time of Coronavirus is being untethered from much of the external influences. Other than Netflix, along with other cable programming, choices are limited. That's helped me and others make choices that feel personally authentic. It allows for a freedom we didn't know possible. Our worlds grew smaller, and our hearts expanded.

Self-Care Tips:

- Find something in your drawers you forgot you have but brings a smile.

- Take a private moment to enjoy something that is fun for you; it could be dancing alone, singing in the shower, or drawing. It doesn't matter if you're good at it or not.

- Get out in the sun and take in the vitamin D.

WEEK FIFTY-NINE:
Culture of Tattletales

"Mommeeeee!" My sister, Susan, yells from our bedroom. "Janet pulled my hair." I hated when Susan tattled on me. Technically, she was right; I did pull her hair, but she failed to share the details of the said pulling. We were playing beauty parlor, brushing each other's curls, pretending to style, paint nails and put on lipstick. Anytime we brush hair we pull it. In the 1960s, we knew of no brushes or combs designed for anything but straight, fine hair. So, putting a brush to

Susan's hair, by definition, meant I was pulling it. Susan was a pro when it came to telling on me. I hated when she did that, because it meant that I would lose another good girl moment to Susan. I would get in trouble even though I meant no harm. I was six at the time to Susan's four.

Now, as an adult, I see similar behavior all the time. People act as if they're four years old, tattling on a sibling who accidentally wronged them. The poor reviews online often seem personal. The writer wants revenge. They didn't like something, and they want to get back at the merchant, the server, the service person. Sometimes I fantasize about getting back at someone. I remember the contractor who almost completed our bathroom. I was angry and thought of going online to write a bad review. Instead, I reached out to him, told him how disappointed I was and that I could not recommend him. He came back and begrudgingly finished the job. He's not someone I'll use again, but I felt good about communicating honestly with him. Last year, I went to a nice restaurant and received mediocre service. I mentioned something to the server. He tried harder, though I doubt he'll ever be a great server. Nonetheless, it was not personal. He just isn't talented as a server. I don't always like speaking up for myself, but it feels better than going behind someone's back to get revenge. If I don't speak up, then the incident or person stays in my mind. By saying something to them directly, there's a better chance I can let it go.

This goes on in workplaces, too. No one wants to speak directly to the person who is causing problems. We go to supervisors, gossip with co-workers, or act out when around the possible offender. We may not always like something, but work and life might be more pleasant if we could communicate with one another about what we don't like. I can complain with the best of them, but do I really need to get a virtual stranger in trouble? Sometimes I want to, but then I think of Susan and remember I was not a happy recipient of her tattling. No need to perpetuate childish behavior. Or, maybe I prefer my righteousness to being a tattletale. Even so, if we all could have the courage to talk to those who upset us, we may experience the possibility of repair.

Self-Care Tips:

- Read the *New York Times* Piece or the book on languishing. It's affirming.

- Let a friend or family member know you're thinking of them. That act of kindness can't be measured, as it's invaluable.

- Speak up for yourself when you have a chance. Give a compliment when someone does something you appreciate. And have the courage to ask for what you want when people get things wrong.

- Go to my website, janetzinn.com, to sign up for the mailing list. I will send a short and sweet newsletter quarterly.

PART II
In the Time of Transition

This section is post-vaccination, partial openings,
and some travel

The world opens up a bit more for all of us

Neither Here Nor There

We are the lucky ones. We have available vaccines that put us in a unique position. We have entered a transitional time from living a life in a deadly pandemic to moving to a new, not fully known, less dangerous, COVID-19 period. So, here we are; we survived, though our experiences remain fraught by what we just endured.

Much of my days look similar to those in the past year. I go to my office, I work, I go for long walks, and I come home to have dinner and rest. The weekends are spent walking and writing, hopefully allowing for some time for fun and still more rest. Though, now, I'm seeing a very small number of clients who are fully vaccinated in the garden of my office, or safely distanced inside. Surprisingly, I found working remotely a nice change from my years of in-person sessions. I hadn't expected that, imagining it would dilute the therapeutic relationship. Instead, it brought new textures to me and my clients' time together. Now I'm finding having in-person sessions a lovely change from Zoom and phone sessions. I enjoy the hybrid of work days that include both in-office along with screen and phone meetings.

All this is to say these middle days, these days of transition, are an odd mix of pre-pandemic routines, pandemic protocols, and new moods and behaviors we've adapted. There is so much we don't know. As a species, we don't do well with the unknown. For me, I stick to what I do know for now. A poorly woven safety net giving me a perceived comfort I so desperately need. It's a bit like wearing a mask that's not completely snug. Or carrying an umbrella in the hope that it doesn't rain.

Let's do our best in moving forward. As we do, let us not forget those we've lost, that which we let go, and the precious lessons we've learned. We will step gingerly while transitioning. The bridge may be long. And, no, we are not there yet.

Self-Care Tips:

- Name the changes you've made during the pandemic that you would like to bring into the future.

- Notice when you're impatient. Rather than get annoyed that you feel impatient, see if you're able to be patient with yourself in your impatience.

- Buy a book from an independent bookstore. If you can't think of what to buy, choose a childhood favorite. It can bring quick comfort when you need it. Of course, if money is an obstacle, see if there's a book exchange or reserve the book at your local library.

Complications of Mother's Day

As a mother and daughter, I find I have such mixed feelings about Mother's Day. Here is one day that's been set aside to celebrate moms. Yet, it has always felt fraught for me. Growing up, I created hand-made gifts for Mother's Day. Excited to present them to my mommy, I could feel her mixed disappointment at the poorly executed drawing or heart-shaped construction paper card. Nonetheless, she displayed these child crafts on the refrigerator so that I could also feel her appreciation for my offerings, lack of craftiness, and all.

Then, year after year, I would hunt stores for gifts that I thought would make her happy. In anticipation of Mother's Day, I felt more anxiety than excitement. Going out for a Mother's Day brunch became a tradition, even if my father couldn't help himself from declaring how high the mark up on the menu was for that one day. For years I would make the trip to my parents' house, fighting for seats on trains and buses from other dutiful children making their pilgrimage to their respective childhood homes.

As a mom, I anticipated the adoration I longed for throughout the year while trying to be the best mother, questioning everything I did, and coming up short because of my own limitations or the limitations of circumstance. I didn't understand yet that the appreciation I desired would have to come from within.

Being a mother and having a mother, or not having a mother, or not fully understanding what motherhood is, all play a part in an often loaded Mother's Day. Mothering ourselves is imperative. I may not always embrace my imperfections, but I can lovingly include them in my makeup. In my sixties, I can finally and continuously be patient with myself while traveling the rugged path I'm on. It's not fair to expect something of others that I cannot give to myself. Therefore, I continue to work on self-care and simple gratitude. Sometimes it's a stretch to be kind to myself if I'm upset and overwhelmed. But it pays off, even if I grudgingly admit it.

This pandemic has tested all our limits. We have discovered more strength in our abilities than we had known before. We have had to discard beliefs we thought were certain. On this second pandemic Mother's Day, having endured difficulties most mothers never imagined, let's celebrate the parent within. The mother in us encourages us to take baby steps toward a life that is deeply satisfying. Remember we're in transition. I might try my hand again at a homemade card. I may never be good at crafts, but I can bring love and laughter to a younger me who resides in my heart. She reminds me of what's in all of us. Happy self-mothering day.

Self-Care Tips:

- Ask yourself, "What is a quality I possess for which I am grateful?"

- What is one thing you can absolutely do today for one minute that reminds you of your inner strength? Take a minute to do that.

- Give yourself a gift dedicated to your inner child and your inner loving parent. Write it, draw it, buy it, think it. Let the gift be good enough.

The Joy & Trepidation of Seeing Smiles

I woke up early and ran to the East River promenade to get a glimpse of the sunrise. I almost forgot my mask, but quickly put it in my pocket, testing the waters of walking down the block without one. No one was wearing masks, but the few of us out were all at least twenty feet apart. That felt comfortable enough for me.

As we all know, the CDC, Centers for Disease Control and Prevention, updated its mask mandate. For a couple of days now, more and more people are on the streets and in the parks maskless. I love being able to see the many faces of the city. Yet, I also feel mask shy. I would have preferred a step-by-step shift during this transitional period. Instead, I'm hearing people mention mask-burning parties. I hear plans to make up for lost time. There is warmth and excitement in the air, as well as a good measure of apprehension.

I may be progressive in my political thinking, but I'm conservative in my COVID-19 opinions. I want more people to get vaccinated, making it safer for all of us. I liked the illusion of security I felt when everyone was wearing a mask. Well, mostly everyone.

My ambivalence is present when I remove my mask to enjoy the aromatic lilacs in the park. I then test the boundaries by walking with my mask on my wrist should I need to quickly don the face covering when others pass by. After exiting a store, I forget to take it off since a more recent habit has me wearing it inside and out.

To quell the mixed feelings, I focus on the flowers in front of apartment buildings, in window boxes, and the beautiful plantings in the gardens and parks. Whatever I may be experiencing, ambivalence and all, Spring colors, longer days, and warmer air all seem to make it easier to get through this time in transition.

Self-Care Tips:

- Stop and smell the flowers.

- Take a walk. Whether you go around the block or enjoy an afternoon stroll, there's nothing like a walk on a Spring Day to feel refreshed.

- Enjoy in-season fruit and vegetables from a farmer's market or farm stand.

WEEK FOUR:
A Wild Time

I was the only adult not accompanying children. The bug carousel was my last stop before exiting the Bronx Zoo. After walking the zoo and enjoying the animals and the respective information on wildlife conservation, I thought, "Why not?" Giving my inner child a treat seemed imperative. Sometimes it just doesn't matter if it makes sense or not.

I've been thinking of new places to go on fun walks. After traversing the same streets, and the same worn paths in the parks, I wanted to shake things up now that it feels COVID-19 safer for me to travel by subway. I'm grateful to the vaccine for that. I chose a weekday, while school was still in session, to enjoy the zoo with fewer people. It was a morning with no clients. When I entered at 10 AM, the opening hour, I walked alone for thirty minutes, seeing zebra, giraffes, and gazelles. Then, for another hour, I saw a few young families while viewing tigers, lemurs, and tropical birds. After that it got busier, so I did my best to go to less traveled areas. As I love elephants, I was able to view Rosie, the Asian elephant out for the day, while I took the monorail, the only way to see her.

It felt delightful to enjoy this space while appreciating these powerful beasts. By the time I made it to the bug carousel, I was ready to sit, even if it meant straddling a sturdy grasshopper going up and down. I went around and around, passing parents and their kids looking at me quizzically. The joy of getting older is that it's easier to choose what's good for me, even if I feel some discomfort in possibly being the object of disapproval. While I risked judgment, I felt the pleasure of caring for myself. All in all, my walk in the zoo was a big gift in this time of transition.

Self-Care Tips:

- Test your courage by doing something for yourself that may risk being judged by others. Make your need greater than what others may think.

- Enjoy animals; whether you play with your pet, go to the park and enjoy looking at a dog run, go to a zoo, or watch silly animal videos on YouTube, animals can often lift our moods.

- Go for a walk in an unfamiliar place. We see things differently, sparking other vicinities of our brain.

No End to Mental Health Awareness Month

We're at the end of May, which is Mental Health Awareness Month. That doesn't mean we can ditch the care we require for our mental well-being. Perhaps now, more than ever, we must hone in on our emotional welfare. As we face many more options than what had been available just a month ago, I find that I am oversaturated with hopes, desires, and hesitation. Listening to my intuition is key, but the noise of opening up, facing all we can do, what we "should do," along with what we'd like to keep from our time in the pandemic, can feel dizzying. I face many choices while I proceed at a low speed.

The challenge is to stay true to my intuition rather than fall face forward into the noise of the world around me. I have been easily seduced by good food, good drinks, good talent, and good times. The pandemic helped to curb some impulses. It helped me to learn to rest more, even as work picked up due to the unexpected global stressors and losses. So, here we are at the crossroads of some semblance of our old lives with what became essential during lockdown.

I'm selfishly relieved that it's a wet holiday weekend. I felt compelled to imagine what I could do during the long weekend. What I really needed was to rest and get some work done. The weather gave me the opportunity to choose what was best for me, rather than delaying the work for fun in the sun. While the time in the pandemic gave me more time to meditate and walk, both of which have been essential self-care, I have to purposely keep those activities in place as the world expands around me.

I love seeing the choices others are making. One of the best mental health benefits of maturing is understanding that I am not obligated to live a life based on others' opinions. I'm not necessarily comfortable when I am in disagreement with plans or interests, but I'd rather endure the discomfort of difference than the discomfort of denying what is right for me. The pandemic allowed my intuition to raise its voice. My mental health is inextricably tied to my listening to my intuition and trusting what it tells me. Now it may be more of an ordeal to listen carefully, but the reward will be a gentle smile from within. My inner self will thank me. What better way to attend to our mental health?

Self-Care Tips:

- Go for a mental health check-up. See your past psychotherapist to check in. Or, find a way to do a self-reflection of what's needed to bring deep satisfaction into your life.

- Access the courage it takes to speak up for yourself while listening to your intuition, rather than ignoring what your gut tells you so that you don't make waves.

- If you're able, take a look at Apple TV's "The Me You Can't See," a show that raises awareness of Mental Illness and Mental Health.

The Charms of a Three-Day Weekend

Memorial Day reminded me of the joy of a three-day week-end. I can always use three days. I don't so much see it as an extra twenty-four hours, as I do experience it as needed time. If we split up the weekend, one day is devoted to accomplishing chores while completing unfinished tasks from the previous week. The next day is for socializing. Whether we catch up virtually or in person, it can be nice to check in with friends and loved ones. And the third day is for much-needed rest. That is what I consider a full and gratifying weekend.

During this current Saturday-Sunday coupling, I am already stressed, attempting to get everything done while staying well-rested. If I want to relieve my stress, then I have to let go of getting everything done and find a way to deal with half a deck. It reminds me of times in my childhood when I'd find pieces missing from games, usually thanks to Susan, my younger sister, who seemed to get great pleasure playing with my toys and ruining them in the process. The red might be missing from Candy Land, or Mrs. Peacock and the lead pipe were nowhere to be found when I took out Clue. I'd find workarounds so that I could finish games, not familiar yet with adult-onset stress.

The simplicity of life during lockdown is waning. Now I'm adjusting to longer to-do lists, adding to daily stress. While I have maintained some anxiety relieving practices, I find that my mind wanders to expanding responsibilities, leaving me with a full mind and lessening my mindfulness. It seems essential to return to the carefree playfulness I had as a child. Should I be able to access a younger me, then I'd easily let go of the missing pieces and continue on with my weekend, such as it is.

I will spend the rest of my Sunday working around a limited time frame. As carefree as my seven-year-old self, I will enjoy the game of life, at least for the next twelve hours, even if it turns out I'm missing a random Jack and the Six of Spades. Apparently, just writing about this is an exercise in letting go. Thanks for playing along with me; you made my weekend.

Self-Care Tips:

- Play. Remind yourself of a younger you who enjoyed a carefree period of time.

- Take dance breaks. Even dancing to one song shifts our energy and allows us to move from stress to ease.

- Throw out old spices. Go through your spice rack and let go of old spices while discovering forgotten spices that will add new flavors to snacks and meals.

WEEK SEVEN:

A Week in the Country

It's heading towards dusk this Saturday evening. We've left the city for a short stay in the Catskills. The air is fresh, the bird songs ever-present. Our arrival was greeted by running groundhogs. On my walk of the vast property, I saw a leaping buck, ducks, yellow, blue, and black with red birds. It feels good to have left the endless concrete for greener pastures. I love New York City and have no desire to reside anywhere that requires driving to get from one spot to another. However, taking a road trip is a nice change of pace.

This time of transition has been a bit overstimulating. I may not be doing the same amount as I had pre-pandemic, but my mind is swimming in new choices. And I'm not alone in that. That is why this time away from my everyday environment is so helpful. I may still be overthinking new possibilities, but I am doing it from afar. In this regard, I am not also looking at every corner to see something I have yet to do or didn't even know needed doing.

I am processing and resting in turns. Finishing this after a night's sleep, this morning is foggy. I had wanted a colorful sunrise but instead was left with a misty grey. Soothing rather than exciting. Tomorrow, rain is upon us. It will literally dampen our plans for hiking. Instead, I may cook, do some yoga, and write. Ease rather than activity. I am not always a go-with-the-flow kind of gal. I like to have plans, mapping out a way to accomplish them. But these two days away give me the opportunity to move away from old habits and adapt to my surroundings. A new lesson in the transition.

Self-Care Tips:

- Slow down. Take yourself out of the clipped pace of your every day and see what that space provides.

- Create something out of leftovers. Give yourself a new take on an old dish.

- Write a list of what you want to maintain from the lockdown, and come up with ways in which you can institute them as things continue to open up.

WEEK EIGHT:
Nothing is Perfect

Happy Father's Day. For all who are fathers or have present and past relationships with your fathers, only you know how best to honor what you're experiencing. And, for those who do not have relationships with your dads, or who have complicated relationships, take care of yourselves. That's all I'll say about that.

I was preoccupied this past week with a few things that didn't quite work out the way I would have liked. You know when you hear people say, "I don't like to complain," and then they're off and running with their objections? I am not that person. I actually like to complain. Truthfully, it's more that I feel compelled to complain than that I like it, out and out. I tend to be very particular, and even when things are going really well, I'm apt to find the fly in the ointment.

We returned from a vacation upstate. Going up, the ride was beautiful once we got into Upper Westchester County. We took backroads after we hit Sullivan County. It's refreshing to see open spaces and green meadows. I am so fortunate to get away. I know that, and I really appreciate it. As a city girl, being in the country is literally a breath of fresh air. I am grateful for a life in the city with these short breaks away from the metropolis.

Social Media posts can seem like someone else is living the good life. Usually, the whole story is that some of it is very good, some not so much. It is often the moral of romances, inspirational tales, and toxic positivity that we should just be grateful. We should only count our blessings. Yet, denying what didn't go well only leaves me stressed and resentful. On this occasion, when I'm able to admit that it wasn't the right rental for us, or that the rain put a damper on hiking, even if I did get the rest I needed, I find relief. Things don't have to be all good or all bad. In fact, they rarely are. Those are the exceptions. In life, good things have aspects that may not be pleasing. So, yes, I will complain, just to name it. Ultimately so I don't hang onto it. Though admittedly, some displeasures stick with me long after the experience. Not so for this short reprieve. We went, we took advantage of the outdoors, and we appreciated the scenery. Past that, I am relieved to be home. Perhaps Airbnb's aren't for me. Or perhaps this one wasn't for me. Either way, I complained and now I'm moving on.

Self-Care Tips:

- Allow yourself to complain about the things that you don't like. It can be a great relief just to name them.

- Hydrate. If water isn't your thing, try adding fresh herbs to give the water a full flavor. Or try something like True Lemon, Lime, or Orange for a fruity finish.

- Give your tired feet a massage.

WEEK NINE:
Happy Pride!

Happy Pride Day. Today our trans son is celebrating. Twenty-four years ago we unwittingly scheduled our wedding on Pride Day. Some friends fittingly missed our straight wedding to celebrate their identity while they marched for their rights. Other gay friends were generous enough to give up their place in the parade to witness our wedding. And everyone had to deal with the traffic that was rerouted to accommodate the crowds and the parade. Larry and I realized then the privilege we enjoyed by being able to get married in 1997.

The world has come a long way since then. It took another fourteen years for same-sex marriage to be legalized in New York State. Yet, in many ways, we have a long way to go. I see this as Alex is enjoying the freedom to be himself among his friends. However, he gets judged in others' company. Not all, but some.

When I was young, I naively believed love would heal

all. I am a true believer in love. And I believe we all have the right to love. But healing often takes love, respect, compassion, listening, non-judgment, hard work, and much more. Love can be a foundation for change, but it's not a one-word solution.

I hope I see a time when all will enjoy the undeniable right of living freely in an accepting world. One in which expression and personal sovereignty are available to all.

Self-Care Tips:

- Take an action for pride month in a way that supports LGBTQIA movements, organizations, groups, or individuals.

- Celebrate summer. Eat seasonal fruits and vegetables, have a BBQ, take a nature walk, or enjoy summer in any way you like.

- Enjoy a summer nap. There's nothing like taking a break in the heat of summer.

WEEK TEN:
July 4th

When I was a child, our family would pack into our Ford station wagon and head out to Pennypacker Park to watch the fireworks. We played in the playground or chased fireflies until the moment when it became dark. Then the night would light up and we cheered with delight as we gazed skyward. It felt magical to enjoy a hot night of colorful pyrotechnics. The crack, pop, and whiz of the fireworks foretold if we'd be seeing a Roman Candle or a burst of high-definition pink chrysanthemum. My favorite was the waterfall, cascading sparkles in the sky.

Tonight, I may skip the fireworks. Fortunate to live in New York City, where the Macy's fireworks grace the darkness over the East River, I am reluctant to stand among so many on the East River Promenade to catch a glimpse of the larger displays. It is not only that we are making our way out of a pandemic; it's more that I don't like myself so much when I jockey to find the right spot and stake my claim. I become territorial and highly suspicious of my fellow humans. Some come with young children, and I turn into an angry older woman, afraid that they will block my view by placing their toddler on their shoulders. Those moments as I wait do not showcase my best self. I am greedy about my space and selfishly competitive with those who only seek an evening of summer recreation.

After spending so much time these past fifteen months learning more patience, and enjoying moments of solitude, I think stepping away from the fireworks will be an act of kindness for myself as well as the nameless strangers who I might secretly hold in contempt. I'd rather bask in my young memories. I was less cynical then. That child in me still feels the awe of the seven-year-old in Pennypacker Park. The sparkle of a childhood recollection reignites the magic of an earlier time.

Self-Care Tips:

- Think of the ways you've grown during the pandemic and find ways to foster that growth as we transition.

- Take a mental health day. If you can't take the day off, perhaps you can give yourself an hour or two. And, if you don't have any time to spare, take a minute to touch base with yourself.

- When things don't turn out how you would have liked, remember to say to yourself, "It's not what I wanted, but it's what I've got." Sometimes it just keeps it real.

WEEK ELEVEN:
Gifts of the Ordinary

This morning was clear and cool enough for summer. My knee wasn't hurting and I could take a slow run by the East River. Ah, a moment of little pain. A small yet welcomed gift when my days are full. Not only could I run after a week of limited walking, but I could enjoy an empty promenade with friendly passers-by. That all added up to a great start to the day.

As we continue to step into a world redefined, it's so easy to want to go back to all we were doing prior to the pandemic. We might miss socializing or live entertainment. Choosing what we do and with whom enhances our sense of continued well-being. And choosing to find the gifts in the ordinary is helpful in our day to day.

I am appreciative of the large flowers gracing our small garden. The smiles and gentle "hellos" are a kindness I so enjoy since I tend to busily move about without seeing individuals. A day without rain brightens the weekend. All these simple gifts deepen my satisfaction. As I can become easily agitated by unpleasantness when I'm feeling raw, I am grateful when I'm in a place in which I can take in the goodness around me.

Ordinary moments are turned into small gems as we amass them throughout the day. They become even more dear because they may be ordinary, but they are not always common.

Self-Care Tips:

- Take stock of the small moments of joy you amass throughout your day.

- Sing to yourself. Notice what you choose. Enjoy it if you can. And, if not, change the station.

- Read good news. Usually, newspapers and other news outlets have pieces that are inspiring, humorous, or just positive.

WEEK TWELVE:
Lazy Summer Days

I still remember my summers visiting friends and family at the Jersey Shore. This was well before Atlantic City was burdened with casinos. These were the days of shows at the Steel Pier and fragrant strolls on the boardwalk, with Mr. Peanut greeting us on our way to James Candy for salt water taffy. Those were the lazy summer days I enjoyed in my former years.

The drive to the beach felt interminable in a car that smelled of stale hot air and shoe polish. My father always carried a wooden shoe shine kit, because "you never know." If we went on a Sunday, then the baseball game was on the radio. As much as I loved going to see the Phillies in person, on our rides down the White Horse Pike, the sports announcers' drone added to the queasy feeling in the back of the station wagon. Once out of the car, I forgot all about my churning stomach and the boredom.

We knew we had arrived when we passed Lucy the Elephant in Margate, two small towns down from Atlantic City with its wicker basket carriages and the divine Kohr's frozen custard. My mother insisted on apples for dessert at home. But all bets were off when in the company of others on the iconic boardwalk. The creamy lusciousness of the chocolate-vanilla twist remains unparalleled.

Summers are so different now. This season, I'm working hard, with weekends assigned to life's ongoing chores. I try to languish. It's true that my walks are more like strolls in the thick air. I feel more tired than lazy. And I'm grateful for having that distinction pointed out to me. Most of us are tired. We have survived a pandemic, and now we're dealing with a more virulent strain. Some of us are critical of ourselves, wondering why we're not more productive, trying to make up for lost time. Yet, it feels necessary to laze. Instead, we can be tough on ourselves. Some are finding themselves restless rather than resting. Nonetheless, it's imperative we create those rare moments in which we can elicit the ease of summers past.

I rarely get to the shore. But when I'm walking in the heat and humidity, I allow myself reminiscences of the sound of the waves mingled with the bustling beaches. Recollecting the aroma of wafting sweetness being churned out behind Kohr's service window.

Self-Care Tips:

- Find a lovely aroma from an earlier time for a sweet remembrance.

- Look at photos, yours or some online, from a place and time that prompts gratitude for having had a special experience.

- Enjoy air conditioning when you can. It can be truly reviving in the heat.

- Give yourself the gift of rest.

Small Moments

When I was in the fifth grade, our teacher, Mrs. Hannah, introduced the idea of a swap lunch. The concept was that mothers (it was 1970) were to create a brown bag lunch, and they would be swapped for a lunch with another student. We picked names out of a hat. As there was an odd number of children in the class, Mrs. Hannah was going to provide a lunch as well. I can't remember who was the recipient of my mother's lunch. But I do recall being mortified. It included a tuna salad sandwich on Pepperidge Farm white bread and an apple for dessert. Not a winning combination.

I was the fortunate recipient of Mrs. Hannah's lunch. It was a thick hoagie, a small bag of chips, a few neatly cut carrots to suggest nutrition and a regular-sized Hershey chocolate bar for dessert. I had never enjoyed such a scrumptious lunch as much as I did that day. It felt as if it was put together with love. And it was all food forbidden on most days in our house. As far as I was concerned, I'd won the jackpot.

At age ten, I worried a lot about being liked. My insecurities were in full bloom. That day with that lunch reassured me more than I could have expressed, that my teacher liked me enough to make a beautiful meal just for me. As one out of four children, and a middle child at that, feeling special was not routine for me. For the most part, I lived in hand-me-downs and was called by one of my sisters' names countless times. So, to be the beneficiary of Mrs. Hannah's meal was a rare moment of joy and gratitude.

In the five decades since then, there have been so many special moments. They range from a huge smile from a stranger yesterday as I walked home, to the many friends who were kind enough to lend me a place to stay when I was a struggling actress in the city. Thank you to Larry J., Phoebe, Michael, Harriet, Astrid, and Jane, to name some of the generous friends to whom I remain grateful.

True kindness is a gift we cherish life-long. I carry so many treasured moments with me. We all do if we let those moments caress us. The arbitrary kindness of friends, family, strangers, and teachers was priceless throughout the pandemic. Benevolence is contagious. Thoughtfulness is always a gift to the giver and the recipient. Thank you to all of you who have brought me a smile, providing a future recollection that helps to make me a better person.

Self-Care Tips:

- Smile to strangers. You never know what a difference it might make.

- Feed someone. Whether you donate to a cause like City Harvest or World Central Kitchen, or whether you choose to send a meal to a friend, food is always a meaningful gift.

- Thank a teacher. Teachers gave so much these last couple of years. The best have always been generous of heart. If you're able to be in touch with a past teacher, or you know a teacher presently, thank them. They work for so little, so a thank you means so much.

WEEK FOURTEEN:
Goodbye to the Old

I'm in my congested closet, trying to decide which of the various multi-colored pocketbooks and bags I'm going to let go. I tend to rely on the same two or three, but I love to choose from the others on special occasions. Of course, there have been very few special occasions in the past year or so. Nonetheless, I had the privilege of attending a joyous outdoor event last night, and though no one else would care, I was so happy to sport the perfect small, blue bag for the evening.

As it turns out I'm not as willing to give up as many bags as I thought. I was able to go through my closet, and doing my own version of Marie Kondo, I let go of anything that no longer brought me joy. Three bags later and I'm feeling a bit lighter. I love the concept of evaluating things based on the joy it provides. It works in so many areas of our lives.

I gave up my gym membership. I prefer movement in my own company or walking with a friend. I was able to downsize my social life so that I could recharge more effectively. Plus, I feel no obligation to continue to read books that aren't right for the time, or watch shows that may be good, but not for me.

All this gives me freedom. I may be busy, but my life is less crowded. My defenses are less fired. As I let go to enjoy more peace, I feel the joy.

Self-Care Tips:

- Let go of something that is joyless this week. It can be a plan you made or an item in the back of your closet. Start small.

- Experiment with doing something differently. Work out with someone if you tend to go solo. Or drink your favorite beverage in a new cup or glass. See if you like the change.

- Muster the courage to disagree with someone who can be forceful. Or, if you tend to voice your disagreement, have the courage to listen quietly, perhaps hearing from a new place.

WEEK FIFTEEN:
Cloudy Mornings

I shifted my routine earlier this week to catch the sunrise. Typically, I relish the space between sleep and daytime. The sweet spot of the morning. Following those moments I shift into meditation, then move on from there with coffee and the rest of the day. As soon as I awoke, I brushed my teeth and ran to the East River to get a glimpse of the sunrise.

It was a cloudy day, and the sun was hidden. No bright colors, just hues of grey. At first, I was disappointed. It's not often I get out to take a peek at the sun coming into view. But then it occurred to me that this was a perfect metaphor for this time in transition. We all want to see the sun but are stuck with grey skies instead. The anticipated bright horizon is more of an idea than a clear vision.

We expected, as we've done in the past, for things to

move along until we could live again as we had pre-pandemic. Instead, we're in this mist. Some of our days look similar to what we've known before, but it's still hazy and not clear enough to navigate straight ahead. We're living in a miasma of uncertainty.

We thought that we would have to endure fear, loss, and ambiguity for a fixed period of time. Then we could face our futures because of these important, albeit unwelcome experiences. We could frame the pandemic with stories of what we've endured, along with life lessons we were forced to learn. But the discomfort has expanded to an indefinite stretch of time. We are still reeling. Our fears remain palpable.

Nevertheless, I am going to continue to look for the sunrise when I wake up too early. And, when the clouds are heavy, I will find simple ways to comfort myself. I'll walk, drink water, read something fun, eat a peach, and rest well. I'll take care of myself as best I can, then I'll see what's needed by those I love, and by those who are in more need. I'll continue to face my days acknowledging my limitations while moving past barriers that keep me stuck. I'll get it wrong and try again. In that way, I keep going while in transition.

Self-Care Tips:

- When you find you're being hard on yourself, think about what you're attempting to learn and shift your focus on the lesson, seeing this moment as part of your learning.

- Remind yourself that it takes time to learn patience.

- Eat a peach or other fresh fruit or vegetables. Summer is a great time to savor the land's bounty.

WEEK SIXTEEN:
Sweet Sixteen

Sweet Sixteen. It doesn't feel so sweet these days. I remember when I was turning sixteen, I yearned to have a fancy party as many of my friends were having that year. We couldn't afford an expensive affair, so I begged and cajoled my parents into allowing me to have a house party. My mother did not enjoy entertaining, nor did she feel comfortable having a good number of adolescents in her home. I didn't realize at the time what a gift she was giving me just by saying yes.

I worked hard to pay for the party, doing overtime to make it happen. I would make runs into Philadelphia to get beads so I could make each guest a personalized necklace. My ambitions were high even though my craft skills were not.

When the party came to be, I remember how uncomfortable I was to bring together my friends from various parts of my life, from Hebrew school cronies to my drama student friend, to those in B'nai Brith Girls (BBG) to old elementary school friends, and my more avant-garde crowd. I was an emotional mess thinking that each knew a part of me, but I was not at ease with myself as a whole and projected quick rejection once they saw the other aspects of my personality. Needless to say, trying to calm my mother pre-party and calm myself took all my energy while setting up.

Each person I invited had a special place in my heart. They had given me their friendship. Not understanding what that meant, I wanted to repay their kindnesses. However, I didn't know myself well enough. I felt fragmented. Sadly, I only remember my discomfort walking indoors and out to make sure everyone had what they needed. Scared they'd find out I wasn't who they thought I was.

It took me decades to learn that our many personality traits are naturally unified. We are and have always been a culmination of the different parts of ourselves.

Last night I had the great fortune of going out for the evening. I was able to meet a Facebook friend from the pandemic for the first time, as well as her awesome sixteen-year-old daughter. My new friend is an extraordinary woman who is bright, sensitive, and fun, among other wonderful traits. Larry was there, as was his friend who has become mine, and his delightful girlfriend. For me, it was a magical evening. Perhaps even more so since there's been a COVID-19 surge, and yet we could still meet for dinner. We don't know what's coming, but in our uncertainty and fear, we made room for laughter and love.

If I think back to my sixteen-year-old self, I don't know that I could have shared my fears if I was supposed to be having fun. Or, I would have missed the fun in deference to my uncertainty. Thank goodness for life experiences that allow us to keep moving forward while honoring the moment. Though I am not grateful for the pandemic and what I thought was this time of transition, I am grateful for new friends, long-term friends, a good husband, and all the other gifts from these many pain-filled months.

Self-Care Tips:

- Make a positive comment online. It can be a compliment for good service, a nice comment to a post, or a short hello to an old friend. It's an easy way to make someone's day.

- Make a note of a life lesson you've learned. Remember how you used to be and recognize how you've grown since then.

- Check in with yourself to see what you need. Sometimes we're preoccupied with what others need, and we don't know if we need rest, if we need to reach out to a friend, or if we need quiet time.

WEEK SEVENTEEN:
Not This!

I remember when I was in my twenties, I took a self-help seminar. I was doing a team activity, and I really didn't like one of the members. She was inappropriately rude, saying things like, "I can feel your anger. Your jaw clenches. It's not pretty. Why don't you just let it go?" Though it enraged me that she would say such a thing, only adding to my ire, I thought I was supposed to become more tolerant of others. So, I pushed my anger down, thinking I was "letting it go," and tried to be accepting of this team member.

It's taken me years to listen to myself and not others' ideas of me. I now see I can respond by saying I don't want someone to speak to me in that way. At the time, I thought I had to carry my shame for allowing my anger to be seen, and I had to hold her insensitive reaction to me. Part of the slow learning curve on my part had to do with not wanting to be where I was. I didn't want to be an angry person. I thought that made me negative. At worst, unlovable. Sometimes I just didn't want to be where I was at any given moment because it was uncomfortable, or it felt intolerable.

Getting through the pandemic has felt so uncomfortable for most of us. Now in this transitional time that has seen a surge of cases, so many have little or no tolerance. We're seeing more impatience, more agitation. We're beat. Collectively we are silently saying, "Not This!" Though we wish this was all behind us, we continue to endure. Repeatedly we are challenged to meet the moment we're in. If and when we look back, we are sadly nostalgic. When we attempt to look ahead, we can feel anxious and hopeless. We might not like these feelings, but they're real. When we deny them because we want to be in a better place, my experience is that those uncomfortable emotions linger. The old adage, "What we resist, persists," is fitting.

If we're able to live with our anger, impatience, boredom, frustration, and exasperation, we can address those feelings. And, in dealing with where we are, no matter how we feel about it, we get to the next moment, and the next. Getting through these difficult times is a moment-by-moment process. Our courage to face ourselves no matter what, more than anything else, allows us to grow in so many ways. Let's meet ourselves at this time with patience, kindness, and care. And, when it's too difficult to muster patience, kindness, and care, let's have extra compassion for living in a difficult space.

Self-Care Tips:

- When having a difficult time, speak with yourself, or write a note as if you were addressing a beloved friend.

- Turn on the music and dance. It can be as short as one song, or make a playlist for a movement break.

- If you're able, balance on one foot. Do it for a few seconds or for longer. It can improve your ability to be in the moment, especially in relation to time and space

WEEK EIGHTEEN:
A Pandemic Birthday

A few years ago, I was at a networking event when I spotted an old acquaintance. I was happy to see her, filled with memories of the two of us with mutual friends enjoying parties, volunteering, and talks in the mid-80s. When I approached her and reminded her who I was, in a cold tone, she responded, "Yes, I know who you are." I felt hurt and dismissed. I thought about those early years in New York City when I couch-surfed and lived hand to mouth. It was a hard time, and I was not always my best self. I had thought warmly of this person, recalling her dedication to friends and her strong work ethic. Her taciturn words indicated she thought less of me.

At first, I blamed myself, thinking I must have been pretty bad for her to have that reaction. Then I thought, yeah, I may have done some crazy things, but I have worked hard to grow and change. I thought how sad for my younger self that I put such a rude person on a pedestal. And then I was proud of myself for my ability to appreciate the positive qualities in others. It doesn't mean I want to befriend everyone. But it does mean that I can respect others and the gifts within them.

This past week I was fortunate enough to celebrate another birthday, though new aches and pains may suggest otherwise. The outpouring of messages and love means the world to me. I feel abundant, filled with gratitude for friends and family who took the time to send thoughtful messages. Taking in the goodness of all of you enriches my life in ways that are difficult to articulate. All I know is that I am better due to you giving your best. What good fortune to be in such good company. I apologize to my younger self for giving authority to those who were unkind. When we're unseen, we cannot be known. I see you and I appreciate you with all my heart.

Self-Care Tips:

- Change it up. Donate to a new non-profit, one aligned with your values but previously not on your radar.

- Provide a simple act of kindness to a stranger. We all need a lift.

- Forgive your younger self for making errors in judgment while he/she/they were learning how to appreciate those who appreciate us.

WEEK NINETEEN:
Are You Okay?

Transitions can be tricky. We usually wish for a straightforward line to the next signpost, but what we often get is a winding road uphill. That is certainly the case these days. This past week is a perfect example of changed plans and tragic outcomes. Water and fire have altered lives irrevocably.

The news is full of sweeping coverage of homes lost and displaced families. In addition, we know of or are hearing of personal stories of loss and vulnerability. I am one of the fortunate ones. I was not in our subway system, and I am not in a flood zone. I hadn't gone on Facebook, so I wasn't aware that we could indicate we were safe. Sometimes I'm just clueless about social media. I'm still uncertain about how to navigate Instagram.

However, some friends and family in other parts of the country, and other parts of the world were so thoughtful in reaching out to see if I was okay. These are simple, caring acts that are deeply appreciated. In my day-to-day, I get caught up in whatever is in front of me. I'm not great about being in touch with friends and family. Sometimes I'm even criticized for it, though I never find that approach inviting.

Life can get very full very fast. But this week taught me that being in someone's heart is not a matter of how many times I've called or written. I so appreciate that. I know it's true for me. Throughout any given week, I recall a moment or a personal exchange with someone I consider close, and I smile. Unbeknownst to them, they provide sustained joy over time.

There have been a good many people who have given their time, attention, love, and humor. I am forever grateful. For that. Thank you to those who reached out to me or to others. It matters. It matters a lot.

Self-Care Tips:

- Send a simple text or IM to let someone know you're thinking of them.

- Play music aligned with your emotions. If you're feeling overwhelmed, play Samuel Barber's Adagio for Strings. If you're a bit playful, listen to Gershwin. Or, if you're wistful, perhaps Aaron Copland will do.

- Look for wonderful nature shots online. There is another Janet Zinn, same name, different person, who is a professional nature photographer. Look her up for beauty and inspiration.

WEEK TWENTY:
Twentieth Anniversary

I'm teary this weekend. It's hard to watch the news because my mind pivots to the many clients who spoke of their losses in the days, months, and years post-9/11. As we commemorate the twentieth anniversary of the terrorist attacks of September 11th, 2001, those of us who remember can clearly recall the exact circumstances when we witnessed or heard of the attacks. I am one of the fortunate who worked downtown, but I had taken the day off to attend a seminar. I never worked in the World Trade Center, but our social service center had a direct view. There were so many other stories like that of those who, for unforetold circumstances were not in the towers when they fell.

I was out of social work school for three years when the planes crashed. Having had training in trauma, but not much experience, I was asked to work with employees in companies who were downtown. It was a quick, intensive training on mental health first response. I had the privilege of listening to individual stories in a new chapter in tragically disrupted lives. Each person I heard had so much courage. They came from all walks of life, surviving while countless loved ones, coworkers, colleagues, and others did not make it.

I recall the kindness and caring that New Yorkers shared. There was a common grace for others. Sadly, I also remember the fear of Muslim friends and those from the Middle East who were harshly judged, misunderstood, or seen as the enemy. Their love of our shared country was unacknowledged. On the one hand, there were so many acts of kindness. On the other hand, there was so much blame going around.

So much sadness, so much anxiety. Both defined the days and months that followed.

Post-trauma can alter our nervous systems. Twenty years later, we're all familiar with that. The last eighteen months have played havoc on our nervous systems. Sometimes we are upset or act out, which then affects others who are in a vulnerable state, and on it goes.

It's a challenge to give someone else the benefit of the doubt when there is so little room to accept our own confused emotions. With practice, we have a bit more patience and a bit more benevolence to get through these days without rushing to judgment of ourselves and others. I cried today. I could have gone on the defensive. Well, I did for a bit, then I cried some more, understanding that vulnerability was the strength I needed to harness rather than residing in a distrustful stance. So many moments leading to big changes.

Self-Care Tips:

- When you react with anger, impatience, or in an accusatory manner, take a moment to ask yourself what might be going on. Then, if you're able, see if there's something you can do to care for yourself. Perhaps a few minutes to regroup.

- Stretch. It's easy. And it can help to move to the next moment with ease.

- Read a child's book or poem aloud. Read it in a voice other than your own. Being silly and indulging in play is a mood changer.

WEEK TWENTY-ONE:
Singing in the Park

As a young child, I delighted in our Magnavox HiFi. I would sit on the scratchy green wool sofa in our den while listening to Rosemary Clooney. Her album, Rosemary Clooney Sings for Children, with its pink background, was a clear favorite. I loved the track, Betsy, My Paper Doll, because I was the lucky recipient of the Betsy McCall paper dolls hidden in the pages of my mother's McCall's Magazine. The other song that spoke to me was The Little Shoemaker because my father was in the shoe business. At six, it felt like Rosemary Clooney was singing to me personally. I hadn't realized Rosemary Clooney was an icon until years later when I watched her sing with Bing Crosby in White Christmas on the Sunday Million Dollar Movie.

Recently, I was reminded of that album while walking in Central and Carl Shurz Parks during this time of transition. On the grass are one- and two-year-olds in a safely distanced semi-circle with their caregivers, listening to Broadway-level singers shaking egg instruments and leading the children in song. They are singing their hearts out to their young audience, who may or may not be singing along. Each performer is grateful for any gig as the theater crawls back from being dark.

How fortunate I was to have enjoyed the musical styling of a great songstress. And how lucky these toddlers are to meet up with some of the best singers from around the country. It's not clear if it's simply a part of their activity schedule or if the family values the influence of music in our lives. Either way, I appreciate walking past them remembering the simple touch of my mother's hand when placing the needle gently on the spinning album, even when I asked to hear it again and again.

In addition to Rosemary Clooney, I heard Lena Horne, Harry Belafonte, Ray Charles, Bobby Darin, Julie Andrews, Judy Garland, and many more who allude my memory, crooning through our oak HiFi. On Sundays, we listened to opera on the classical radio station. That's when my grandparents visited. We all sat quietly on the same itchy green sofa or love seat. If we couldn't be quiet, we had to go play in the basement. I favored Puccini and Mozart. The songs felt pretty to me. But not having an album cover to attempt to read was a limitation that had me go to the basement after an aria or two.

I'm not listening to enough music these days. It's time to open up iTunes and delight in Rosemary Clooney and friends.

Self-Care Tips:

- Play music you used to enjoy. Take in the memories and notice how the songs and music impact you now.

- Take a walk and see what associations you conjure. What recollections come to mind?

- Create new memories by sharing music with someone you respect. If possible, listen together. If you can't, you can enjoy the association with the music.

WEEK TWENTY-TWO:
Popularity Contest

Over fifteen years ago, I organized a networking event for psychotherapists and others in related fields. I hosted it in my office garden and prepared a beautiful buffet of crudité and homemade dips and finger food. I received a lot of maybes, and about fifteen said they would attend. Of course, I overestimated and prepared too much food. In the end, I had five guests; two just stopped by.

It was an intimate event. The four of us who stayed were able to appreciate and understand what each of us offered clients, and it ended on a positive note. However, I was mortified that more people didn't come. I was embarrassed for myself and felt I let my colleagues down. It was challenging to stay focused with the other women who came. Instead, I spent too much energy focusing on who wasn't there.

It harkened back to parties in elementary school and

junior high to which I was never invited. Or times when the red rope was not unhooked for me at Studio 54 and the Palladium. The rejection felt personal. I was not one of the chosen ones.

Since those times, I realize I do better in small groups or one-on-one. I get too distracted at large parties. Yet, as I currently work on a book, mostly on odd weekends, I have been told by so many that I need a platform. That means that I must amass followers and readers. I always feel awkward when asking others to read my work. Larry, my husband, may be the exception.

I like writing, but I don't like marketing for myself. It feels too much like my ten-year-old self asking to be liked. No, thank you. I will continue to create this book on getting through difficult times with self-care tips, slowly and painstakingly. I don't know if I'll get an agent or get it published. Nonetheless, I will proceed, trusting that I don't need to be someone I'm not just to be popular. It is not in my best interest to consider numbers rather than you, dear reader.

Self-Care Tips:

- Affirm that you are enough. Write "I Am Enough" on post-its and place one on a corner of your bathroom mirror, and other places you view daily (inside a drawer, on your refrigerator door, etc.).

- Learn a new song. It can be easier to remember things put to music. So learning a new song is a great way to exercise your brain.

- Remind yourself that bigger is not necessarily better. When plans change and you have a smaller event (as in these past eighteen months), find the sweetness in the intimacy of the experience.

WEEK TWENTY-THREE:
Getting Away

Sometimes we just need to get away. It helps to clear our heads and take a break from day-to-day stress. That's exactly what we did this weekend. It's been a long time coming. I booked this trip before the pandemic shut down our world. I rebooked three times in the hope that quarantines were a temporary inconvenience. In the end, we had to wait until the Canadian border opened up for the fully vaccinated.

I was nervous to take my first big trip out of the country. But I also wanted a proper vacation. It felt like I needed a proper vacation. So here we are in Quebec City, fully enjoying the hospitality and food that is offered with care.

The joy of walking unfamiliar streets and seeing the colors change on the trees has proven to be just the break I needed.

Self-Care Tips:

- Take a break. If you can't get away, give yourself quick moments throughout the day when you take five deep breaths for a short pause.

- Start taking note of the colors changing on the trees. What colors do you like the most? Which trees look as if they're ablaze? Enjoy the richness of the season.

- Savor the natural foods of the season. Whether you like all things pumpkin, or you're an apple fan, the flavors of fall offer so much.

A Rare Moment of Calm

I hit the ground running. There was so much to get done, and I'm still behind. I did the best I could, which means I had to readjust from vacation mode to New York City-paced backlog catch-up. Within a few days, the vacation glow is flickering.

Sometimes, getting away is the space needed to re-evaluate what works and what doesn't. There's no way I can keep up my current pace. What goes? Time will tell.

The idea of living simply makes perfect sense. I can be still when meditating. The quiet time before my coffee is delightfully simple. The rest of the day is a maze of work, calls, paperwork, walks, family time, dog time, emails, and, if I have the energy and a rare opening, a good TV program.

It took me until today, while walking Lucy, to appreciate the cool air on the East River Promenade, without my phone, without a podcast, and without distraction. Just Lucy and I strolling along. When I was away, I was able to go for swims. I love the tranquility of an empty lap pool. Though I have yet to find a quiet pool in the city, my walks with Lucy brought calm to my otherwise hectic days.

Self-Care Tips:

- Find a new book, TV program, movie, or something you can enjoy at the end of busy days.

- Try to go for a quiet walk without a phone or other interference. Notice what it's like to move peacefully.

- Play the make-believe drums with spatulas and pots. Get out all your frustration by tapping into your inner child, pretending to be a rock star.

WEEK TWENTY-FIVE:
Hello Sunrise

When I was a young child and my bedtime was 7:30, the advent of a darker evening meant that I was awake longer while the night sky became opaque. It felt as if I was staying up later, even though I understood, in theory, I was going to bed at the same time. Since the pandemic, my bedtime has gotten earlier. I go out less, plus I got older these past nineteen months. I have yet to go to bed at 7:30, but it feels easy to get into bed when it's been dark for a few hours.

The advantage to this is that the sun rises later, giving me a chance to wake up with time for coffee and a very short walk to the East River promenade to get a picture of the morning's dawn. I love how frequently the light changes from moment to moment and from day to day. While our world has changed in so many ways, I appreciate the regularity of the sun. Even on cloudy or rainy days, the sun may not make an appearance, but trusting it resides behind the clouds gives me great comfort.

There is a simple joy in recognizing the beauty in nature. While a city girl at heart, getting away, or finding the green patches among the concrete, is a balm for the soul. The cool weather sunrises, and when possible, the sunsets provide a colorful array of grace. Those moments have been invaluable in bringing ease during these tenuous times.

Self-Care Tips:

- Enjoy sunrises and sunsets. If you don't have a view of them, there are amazing pictures online. Thank you to those who post such gorgeous photographs.

- Ground yourself by standing on grass, rocks, or other solid earthbound foundations. Feel your feet connecting to the earth. Stand tall so that you feel as if the crown of your head is extended from an invisible cord skyward.

- If your schedule permits, allow the early dark evenings to ease you into a sense of restfulness.

WEEK TWENTY-SIX:
Funny Thing About Gratitude

I find it incredibly annoying when I'm upset about a person, place, or thing. I'm on a rant, and the individual listening responds by telling me I should be grateful. It feels like a dismissal of my complaint, valid or not, and a recommendation that I pivot to a "soft music inserted here" blissful moment when I see how lovely life is and how wrong I was to find the awful in this grand world we inhabit.

I see the benefits of complaining. I find it helps me to release my frustration, as well as other unpleasant emotions, so that I can find that blissful place on my own. I am all for being inspired, but I am not a fan of skipping the messy parts so that I make it easier for someone else.

Conversely, in moments of awe and wonder I enjoy the wave of gratitude that envelops me. And, in times when

I experience hardship, and my family, friends, acquaintances, and/or strangers offer their support, I am forever grateful. Kindness is taken in and helps me to grow. My heart softens.

When I listen to award shows, I feel bad for the winners who only want to share their special moment by acknowledging the countless others who allowed them to reach that stage, but the orchestra music plays to interrupt them. Though I won't name names here, only because I am apt to miss some, I am forever grateful to my relatives, friends, teachers, mentors, therapists, co-workers, colleagues, classmates, and others who have shared their thoughtfulness. It has inspired me. Their acts of kindness have been invaluable whether they remember them or not.

So, if, for a short time, I complain, it is only so that I can unload on my own terms, allowing me to get back to a place in which I am genuinely grateful for all the times I've been the recipient of your and others' generosity of heart.

Self-Care Tips:

- Find a person to whom you can share your complaints. In the absence of a neutral listener, write down your complaints so they are not swimming in circles in your brain.

- Remember times in which you were the recipient of arbitrary kindness. Check in with how it feels to recollect that time.

- Write a thank you note. We have lost that art, and they are so appreciated.

WEEK TWENTY-SEVEN:
Happy Halloween

The first time I wore a mask, I was three years old and was aware of the tiny holes for my nostrils and the slit for my mouth. Not easy breathing, but so exciting to this little girl. I was a cat, Felix the Cat, to be precise. My one-piece, highly flammable costume had a small tie in the back of the black and white jumpsuit. I held a small paper bag for my trick-or-treat goodies next to my sister Sharyn and my dad, who came home from work early to escort us up and down our New Jersey suburban block.

I loved Halloween. Getting dressed up and pretending to be someone or something else was good with me. Plus, it was the one time in the year in which I had my own candy. In those days, the early 60s, candy cigarettes and dots on paper were my favorites, with Hershey kisses a close second.

I will not be dressing up this Halloween. Instead, I will watch children donning costumes, purchased and homemade, in strollers and in small groups as they accept the offerings from the businesses on the avenues. I will not venture downtown to witness the Halloween parade, a more crowded and less innocent affair than when I came to the city in the 80s. The only mask I'll be wearing is some colorful number from my new mask drawer, thanks to the pandemic.

I'm not big on horror films or scary things in general. My view is that there is enough to frighten us on a daily basis. I don't need to purposely activate that fear. But I give a pass for Halloween, appreciative of all the city dwellers who decorate their homes for the pleasure of passers-by. Whether you dress up or not, wishing you a Happy Halloween, a very nice Sunday, or both.

Self-Care Tips:

- Wake up early, when possible, to get one thing done that will help start your day.

- Sleep in when possible and enjoy a slow morning.

- Watch or read something that eases your fears, like a light comedy or an inspirational tale.

WEEK TWENTY-EIGHT:
Time for a Marathon

Time is a funny thing. If we sleep late this morning, we wake up at our regular time due to daylight savings time. The fall back of the time change here in New York City is particularly fortuitous for the NYC Marathon runners in the event they could sleep at all.

Today I'll be cheering from the sidelines. I am always moved by the determination and grit that it takes to run a marathon. I am deeply inspired by each marathoner. The early runners are great athletes who race to win. The Achilles Club athletes, some accompanied by guides, always move me, often to tears, because they transcend physical and mental barriers to get through the 26.2 miles to the finish line. And the other runners, joggers, and walkers among the 30,000 total NYC marathoners this year who trained to be able to move through the five boroughs of our city.

A shout out to my friends Julie, Jeannette, and Debbie, who I will be tracking to cheer them on at East 87th Street, close to my office. They all trained for two years since the only options last year were solo, virtual runs. This year they'll all start from the lineup at the Verrazano Narrows Bridge in Staten Island. Their first step carries them through all that follows.

I am proud to have run the NYC marathon six years ago. I was not a runner. I learned to run slowly to manage physical limitations, including shortness of breath. It was hard to find a trainer for this type of running since most marathon trainers focused on minimizing running times while emphasizing form. So, without formal training I found the best way I could do it, slow and steady. All those cheering from the sidelines gave me the stamina to keep going. I am eternally grateful to my friends, family, and strangers whose enthusiasm provided me with energy.

Whether we can make it out to the marathon course to cheer the runners on, or whether we encourage those in our lives to follow their dreams, we may never know the full power of our support. Again and again, we hear of those who have had major accomplishments and thank parents, teachers, mentors, and friends for the support they received from them. Let us all take the time, in much of the USA where we now have that extra hour, to support someone in reaching his, her, or their dreams. And, whether you're running a marathon or reaching for your marathon equivalent, have the courage to ask for support. It will move you forward in countless ways.

Self-Care Tips:

- Run around the block. Run slowly. Notice if this run feels different than the other ways you move.

- Take one step to start something new today. Observe what it takes to take that first step. You may be pushing yourself. Take note if this step feels productive. Do you feel you accomplished something? Do you feel hopeless that you can keep moving in the direction of completing it? And do your feelings tell you something about it that is useful?

- Find the people or circumstances that inspire you. Pursue ways that you can regularly feel inspired. It awakens something deep in us.

Don't Get Caught With Tattered Underwear

I was doing my laundry last week. While hanging my underwear on the hand dryer, I noticed the rips that must have happened over time, the time spent quietly during the pandemic. Everything was so comfortable, so I never stopped to examine them. And comfort has been key. Though comfort still matters, I'll take my underwear without rips.

While I was choosing my new briefs, which I was thrilled to find on sale, I was thinking of the last time tattered undies played a role in my life. It was twenty-five years ago. I was walking to work, crossing the street, when a cabdriver turned the corner without looking. He hit me and lifted me onto his bumper until he stopped suddenly, and I slid down onto the cold street.

An ambulance came and checked on me. I didn't know

I was in shock, but I wouldn't let them take me to the hospital. I insisted I'd go to my doctor's office. I went, but only after I returned home to call work. This was before everyone had cell phones. After I made that call, I searched through my undergarment drawer to find at least one pair that was worthy of a doctor's visit. I was not putting on an examining gown with torn granny panties. Since that time, I've made it a point to have accident-ready underwear. I see it as a preventative measure.

The truth is I learned a lot more than to avoid torn clothing. The accident and the months following really taught me to take care of myself in a more conscious way. The first steps were to heal from the accident. Thanks to good physical therapists, medical massage therapists, an acupuncturist, medical specialists, and my psychotherapist, I got through the pain to the other side. I was lucky. Not only did I have good insurance, but I also had good care.

There was so much more to learn. Being prepared for the unexpected was not part of my toolbox. Through the years I've learned patience. I learned how to pivot when needed. Being flexible, even if I inwardly resist change, has been invaluable. It took the pandemic to teach me to slow down. Slowing down helps when the world turns upside down. It even helps as the world, step by step, turns back around with an unfamiliar view.

For now, getting new underwear is a fresh start in this changing world.

Self-Care Tips:

- Slow Down. It seems like there's always something to get done because there usually is. But slowing down gives us a perspective that we don't get when we're speeding ahead.

- Ask yourself what act of kindness will help you prepare for the unexpected. Change is a given. Having patience and kindness for ourselves when we face the unknown brings a bit of peace when we may be inclined to stress.

- If you're able, indulge in a new pair of underwear. And throw out one that is no longer comfortable for you.

Thanks Giving & Thanks Getting

We're about to ascend upon Thanksgiving and the winter holidays. I'm grateful for a quiet dinner with Larry and a restful weekend. I've been looking forward to this coming weekend since rest is usually ad hoc, and I am often trying to locate windows of opportunity to relax.

There's a lot written on the power of gratitude. It's the cornerstone of positive psychology and Western mindfulness practices. My life has changed significantly by incorporating a daily gratitude practice. When I was younger, I felt like a victim. I looked at hard circumstances as a reflection of my inability to manifest a better life. It was a form of self-criticism that could be relentless. Though I enjoyed fun times, my focus was on what I hoped to have or what I didn't have. Mostly, it was a deprivation mindset. And, if something good came my way, but it didn't meet my expectations, I would be crestfallen. Needless to say, this was so frustrating for those close to me.

Now, I've probably moved too far in the other direction. I acknowledge the good in my life. However, sometimes I omit how hard it's been. That can feel inauthentic.

I admit, these have been a hard couple of years. And, despite the difficulties, there have been beautiful walks throughout the city. The pandemic taught me the importance of rest. We moved. I now have a daily view of the sun rising. Larry and I are communicating better, thus enjoying each other more. Our trans son, Alex, who began the medical transition a year ago, though it was many years in the making, is finding his way in the world. His transition is ongoing. I have amazing friends. And I started this blog at the start of the pandemic. I am grateful.

It's more of a stretch to be grateful for health concerns, expanding mental health needs in the city and the world. I'm not grateful for growing inflation, though I do appreciate my ability to edit shopping lists by asking myself, "Do I really need this?" What a mixed bag we're in. Nonetheless, if we focus on the small victories and if we have the courage to find the good among those who are angry and dissatisfied, we can move forward rather than being held back. Rather than imposing forced gratitude on those around us, let's share our thanks for what they contribute to us. Give thanks while letting others get thanks.

Self-Care Tips:

- Simply say thank you the next time you're complimented. Stay with the gratitude the person or people shared while enjoying the exchange.

- Find small moments that bring deep satisfaction. It can be a private moment, or it can be shared. Either way, take it in. Breathe.

- Write a Thank You note to yourself. What has made you proud? Can you be grateful for trying? See if you can appreciate the positive you bring to your life.

Thank You
Mr. Sondheim

I was working at Strawbridge and Clothier in the Men's shoe department. This was a branch in the Echelon Mall in Voorhees, NJ, a short commute to Philadelphia. I was a student at Rutgers University in Camden, still a theater major, though I would finish with a degree in English. Paul Puccio, an English major at another college who worked in Men's Furnishings, introduced me to the music of Stephen Sondheim. I was eighteen years old. He was enamored with Follies and Alexis Smith. He invited me over to his home, where I listened to his original Broadway cast album with Paul narrating to a neophyte. I was changed for life.

The year was 1978. I had never heard anything like it. My New Jersey suburb was not void of art, but I hadn't been privy to the musical stylings Yof Stephen Sondheim until then. The next year I would take a Trailways bus to

New York City to see Sweeney Todd. I was enthralled. The double entendre, the dark humor, the rhythmic pattern, and the soulful harmonies. I would finish out my college years living in Philadelphia, listening again and again to a turntable set on one Sondheim musical or another.

Part of my impetus for moving to Manhattan post-graduation was to be able to attend any and all Sondheim shows. I sang his songs with great longing in the shower or at a voice lesson. I did not possess the vocal quality to perform his songs in public. Yet, I happily enjoyed being an audience member for many shows, including the 1995 revival of Company, in which the versatile Debra Monk gives her powerful rendition of The Ladies Who Lunch. More recently, I thoroughly enjoyed the stellar cast of the current production of Assassins off-Broadway.

Stephen Sondheim died Friday at the venerable age of ninety-one. I am grateful for his provocative musicals. Every revival has allowed me to learn something new from his intricate music and lyrics. I am one of so many who repeatedly metabolized the Sondheim oeuvre. Students, audience members, theater professionals, and fans from around the world have their own poignant Sondheim connections. He was a legend. We were fortunate enough to live in a world in which his work could touch our souls. Thank you for Being Alive, Mr. Sondheim.

Self-Care Tips:

- Go to YouTube and enjoy the many stars who interpret Sondheim songs. Some suggestions are Raul Esparza, Debra Monk, Elaine Stritch, and Barbara Cook.

- If you're able, get tickets to see Assassins at The Classic Stage Company, and/or Company on

Broadway. If not, find out when there is a local or college production of a Sondheim musical near you.

- Croon in the shower or anywhere you can sing from your heart.

WEEK THIRTY-TWO:
Looking Back

I had some ideas about what I'd be addressing for this blog post, but when I looked at my calendar, I saw that it's been four years since my mother died. We had a complicated relationship. Yet, in the last year of her life, as her health declined, we found common ground with a deep and enduring love. A time I will always treasure. Most people don't get that opportunity. Understanding that death is inevitable, her dying days were filled with peace and love.

In the ensuing years, I have come to appreciate the many things I learned from her. Good manners matter. Respect privacy, one's own and others' need for discretion. Appreciating those who share kindness in the world. A love of tennis and figure skating. A love of salads. And an understanding that we do not really know what others are going through, so perhaps we can give them the benefit of the doubt.

In the song from Jerry Herman's Mack & Mabel *Time Heals Everything*. I am grateful for all I learned in that relationship and how it translates time and again in my life. Sadly, this week, I found out a friend younger than me died. He was such a giving and caring man. I am so grateful for his support and care for almost forty years. I will take those experiences, too, into my future.

As we come to the final weeks of 2021, let's reflect on the ups and downs of a pandemic year and what lessons can be culled from this time. Who is no longer in our lives? What did we learn from them? In what ways have we let go? How have we changed? How have we endured?

I'm not sure I'm any stronger than before. But I do have a recognition of my strengths that were unacknowledged before the pandemic, and certainly before my mother's death. What I know now is that this is my life, my journey, no matter what others think. Partly, it's a realization born out of getting older. Partly, it's a gift provided by witnessing my courageous clients and how uniquely each of us finds our way back to ourselves.

Wishing you peace and love as we see the end of this complicated year.

Self-Care Tips:

- Make a list of the ways you've grown this past year. Acknowledge yourself for that growth.

- Think of those who are no longer in your life, whether by death, other circumstances, or by choice, and make note of how you've changed because of those relationships.

- Think of what you will let go of before 2022 arrives. Write it down, and then burn the list, rip it up, or find your own way of releasing it.

WEEK THIRTY-THREE:
We Are Not Okay

I'm finding this holiday season to be quite odd. On the one hand, many of us are able to travel, visit with friends and family, and celebrate the holidays in person rather than on Zoom. On the other hand, our nervous systems have been taxed beyond what we thought possible as we forge ahead.

I so appreciate the invitations I've received for in-person celebrations. And, yet, I just don't feel up to it. I am less inclined to have small talk. I like to see people, but not much is new in terms of life changes, and I don't have the wherewithal to listen even though I'm interested. So I sit out the parties. Parties I yearned to attend in my twenties and thirties. Parties I will forego in my sixties while we still cope with a pandemic.

When we ask, "How much more can we endure?" we're simply given more. Plodding ahead, a bit slower than before. Sometimes I can delight in a small moment, such as walking with a friend or enjoying a chance to meet in Central Park. Other times I am enraged by what would seem an insignificant event.

Today my face burned as I attempted to walk around a family who abruptly stopped in the middle of the sidewalk to adjust something in their stroller. It wasn't an emergency, and they had plenty of room had they cared to walk a couple of steps, moving closer to the curb. I have little patience for those who are not considerate of others. Simple kindnesses go a long way. I soften when someone is gentle or thoughtful. Later in the day, a neighbor helped me with a package, and I could have cried from gratitude. Ambivalence and a general malaise have ruled these last months. It's kind of like a throwback to my adolescence, or maybe even menopause. Two stages I would have preferred to leave in the past. Yet here I am, moody and grateful.

Self-Care Tips:

- Smile to a stranger. Know that they, too, are going through a lot.

- Allow yourself to slow down. It's easier to make room for your feelings, your process, or anything you're experiencing when you slow down, take a breath, and say, "In this moment, this is where I am."

- Take a bath. If you can, find some bath soap paint that washes away. Create art on your body in the tub, then wash it away. It's fun, and it will be a reminder of the impermanence of our situation.

WEEK THIRTY-FOUR:
Generosity of Spirit

I always thought I was a generous person. Then I got married and I came to realize that I was only generous in certain circumstances. If something was my idea, great, I was happy to offer services, a gift, or lend an ear. However, if asked, I found I could be withholding. Somehow I felt being asked for something implied I was stingy. And I was. Sometimes I still am. Apparently, a generous heart is not a one-way endeavor.

I started to notice that "no" was my immediate response when asked for something. I had to learn to pause to see why. I didn't like this stingy quality and wanted to do better. What I found was that I had often volunteered or ignored my needs to give in ways that, more often than not, were a sacrifice. I ignored my own needs to unconsciously gain acceptance from others. Once I stopped giving in those instances, I had more room to give of myself at other times. I felt less resentful and less parsimonious.

Holidays often highlight our generosity or lack thereof. If we're motivated by a giving heart, we will feel the joy of the season. If we receive with a generous spirit, we take in so much more than the gift at hand. And, yet, we've been through a lot. Having foregone so much, with more closures happening at present, we might feel particularly challenged to access our generous spirit.

As we traverse the Omicron variant surge, let's do our best to open our hearts to one another. We're in for a bumpy ride. I'm going to do my best to find the humanity for those who make me bristle. I will be testing myself. Do I have the grace to live and let live? Or will I be judging others? Seething through a tight jaw.

I don't know what will show up when I'm stressed or down. But I'll use my reactions as measures of what I might need in terms of grace. And, then, I'll do what I can to have patience as I move through the end of this difficult year into a new year in which living in the spirit of generosity will serve me more than holding on.

As we open ourselves up to the many gifts in life, may we all benefit from the act of giving and receiving.

Self-Care Tips:

- Send thank you notes. It means so much to those who give to us to know that the gift was received in the spirit of generosity.

- Stay within your budget. It can feel challenging to not overspend. Remember that an act of love can mean so much more than a boxed gift paid on credit.

- Regift to places that accept new items for those who might have lost so much. Some places you might consider are domestic abuse shelters, tornado victims, and emergency immigrant centers.

So Long 2021

2021 was so, so long. In this last week I have little interest in reviewing this past year. The fact that I, that we, got through it is good enough for me.

The good news is that not looking back, at least for now, keeps me in the moment. My quandary is whether I've chosen mindfulness or denial. If I choose mindfulness, then there's space for my denial. If I go with a state of denial, then who cares? I will not decide. I will opt for a "both/and" rather than an "either/or" scenario.

The effort that goes into a binary dilemma is too great. We spend so much attention making an argument for our point of view. The more I defend a specific position I take, the less likely I am to learn something new.

So long, 2021. I will not miss you. I appreciate much from this past year. Larry and I moved to a nicer home. We didn't know we could do it, yet here we are. I continue to enjoy a hybrid private practice, in-person and virtually. Three hundred sixty-five sunrises and sunsets made for beautiful light. Being in touch with friends and family, when possible, brought love and laughter. Reading new essays, books, and articles enriched me. Not finishing books, no matter how highly praised by critics, was pure relief. And daily walks always expanded my vision. For those and many other gifts, I am grateful.

However, having to reach into our depths to get through a full year of the pandemic unnerved most of us. Our tempers were shorter, and our patience wanting. We are at the final stretch. It's less than a week until we ring in the new year. For me, it will be less of a new beginning than it will be a step forward. Another step into the unknown.

Self-Care Tips:

- Take the pressure off New Year's Eve or New Year's Day. If you have plans, have fun and stay safe. If you don't have plans, enjoy the simplicity of staying in.

- Rather than making New Year's resolutions, think of what you might like to let go of.

- Regift. If what you received isn't for you for any reason, find those around you who would appreciate it. Or donate. Either way, it's a win-win.

Conclusion

Thank you so much for taking this journey with me. It's not always easy looking back. There are repeated themes, lessons, and self-care tips. They mirror the repeated challenges I faced. They also speak of the importance of repitition in our personal growth processes. When we remember what we've been through, we can appreciate what we have. And we value our courage and strength in getting through hard times. We're able to access compassion for ourselves and others, realizing that we all have meaningful stories that shape us.

If you picked up this book for the self-care tips, be sure to tailor them to your needs. Remember that what supports us in one situation may not be right in different circumstances. Yet, you may find that there are some tried and true self-care recommendations that fill out your self-care tool kit. Whatever your needs, I'm hopeful that you can find tips to suit you.

I wish you well on your journey ahead, and I am grateful you paused to look back while reading **In the Time of Coronavirus**.

ACKNOWLEDGMENTS

Thank you to Jan Van Zant, who has supported me from the very first blog post. Thank you so much to my sister, Sharyn Feldman, who has shared and supported my posts. And to her brother-in-law, Steve Rubio, who has been a devoted follower from the beginning. Thank you to my son, Alex Zinn, for proofreading as well as sharing posts. Thank you to my writing teacher, Charles Saltzberg, who has been an encouraging mentor for years as I learned how to write and, maybe more importantly, how to rewrite. And, thank you to all the fellow students in his workshops who shared their writing and comments so I could learn to write better. Thank you to Jeannette Sanderson and Beth Leibson who, in class and out, supported my writing. Thank you to Erin Falk and Nicole Wegweiser, who both suggested I turn my blog posts into a book.

Thank you to my therapist, Marcia, who has patiently watched me through the ups and downs and has made room for me to learn and grow. Our relationship has been priceless. Thank you to Lela Zaphiropolous, who has uplifted me and my clinical work and for whom I am eternally grateful.

Thank you to Candace Coakley, who was a caring publishing coach, and who pointed me in the direction of Atmosphere Press. Thank you to Phoebe Collins who generously proofread. My gratitude to my first proofreader, Lavinia Kajura. My deep appreciation to Caryn Leigh Posnansky who created the author portraits for this book at Caryn Leigh Photography. I am so grateful to Ronaldo Alves and his team for designing the stunning book cover. And thank you to all the staff at Atmosphere Press, including Alex Kale, Kyle McCord, and Tammy Letherer.

Thank you to my husband, Larry Zinn, who has lovingly been there every day before, during, and following the COVID-19 pandemic. Thank you to Jodi Karp for the parallel walks, as well as personal and professional support throughout the pandemic and beyond. And thank you to Lisa Schwebel for her constant encouragement and friendship.

I am eternally grateful to my clients, past and present, who have allowed me to witness their courage and growth as they work to improve the quality of their lives while inspiring others to live their best lives. Each one is a hero in their respective lives.

ABOUT ATMOSPHERE PRESS

Founded in 2015, Atmosphere Press was built on the principles of Honesty, Transparency, Professionalism, Kindness, and Making Your Book Awesome. As an ethical and author-friendly hybrid press, we stay true to that founding mission today.

If you're a reader, enter our giveaway for a free book here:

SCAN TO ENTER
BOOK GIVEAWAY

If you're a writer, submit your manuscript for consideration here:

SCAN TO SUBMIT
MANUSCRIPT

And always feel free to visit Atmosphere Press and our authors online at atmospherepress.com. See you there soon!

ABOUT THE AUTHOR

JANET ZINN, LCSW, is a psychotherapist in private practice in New York City. As soon as COVID-19 was detected in the USA, it became apparent that anxiety was on the rise, and fear was leading the way into our collected psyches. Having been a mental health first responder following 9/11, and as a psychotherapist who specializes in trauma, loss and crises, Janet started blogging as a way to bring self-care suggestions in the form of tips and tools so that readers could find a way forward in that difficult time. In addition, the blog posts shared Janet's own struggles and perspectives during those first months so readers' experiences could be normalized by a shared understanding.

Janet is inspired by her clients. She watches for trends in what is needed in mental health. And she is moved daily by the courage and grace her clients exhibit when facing adversities. After she started the blog, *In the Time of Coronavirus*, Janet was further motivated by the reactions and feedback she received from her readers. Thus, this book was created.

She is currently a member of The Women's Mental Health Consortium, a prominent New York-based community of mental health providers. She was previously a faculty member of the Women's Therapy Centre Institute. As a mental health first responder following 9/11, Janet ran groups and met individually with every level of employee, from CEOs to security guards at Fortune 100 companies, as well as at smaller firms, non-profit organizations, and small to mid-sized corporations. She consulted as a trauma specialist on-site at Fortune 100 companies for over five years.

Janet is an international speaker on trauma and consulted at the beginning of the pandemic in Australia. She has been featured as a trauma expert on Swedish Public Television. She has led international virtual training sessions for top executives on 9/11 anniversaries for Goldman Sachs and Citigroup. She supervises mental health students and professionals as they counsel various populations of all age groups, vulnerable populations, those who have faced discrimination, and victims of crimes, all of whom are dealing with trauma. She worked as a trauma consultant for New York City banks following bank robberies from 2001 to 2010.

Janet Zinn has been quoted in *The Times of London*, *The New York Times*, *The Washington Post*, *Marriage* ezine, WebMD, *Healthline*, *Bustle*, and other online and print publications. She was the relationship counselor doing therapy sessions, taped live for XOX Betsey Johnson, a reality TV show on the Style Network.

Currently, she is a blogger. Her blog posts can be found on https://janetzinn.com, as well as on Medium and WordPress. She started the ongoing blog, *In the Time of Coronavirus*, which is now called *In the No Longer New Abnormal*, providing a mindful approach to life's post-pandemic challenges and a versatile menu of self-care tips. Janet blogs in tandem with her full-time private psychotherapy practice. Janet has a B.A. from Rutgers University and an MSW from New York University. She has post-graduate certificates from Fordham University, The Women's Therapy Centre Institute, and The International Trauma Specialists Association. For *In the Time of Coronavirus*, Janet shares experiences, professional insights, and the tools necessary to live authentically through all of life's ups and downs, with an eye for what we collectively experienced, finding meaning in those times, as well as a way forward.